FOR THE LOVE OF COOKING

FOR THE LOVE OF COOKING

by

Rae Dayan

TARGUM/FELDHEIM

First published 2000
Copyright © 2000 by Rae Dayan
ISBN 1-56871-167-0

All rights reserved

No part of this publication may be translated, reproduced, stored in a retrieval system, or transmitted in any form or by any means, electronic, mechanical, photocopying, recording, or otherwise, without prior permission in writing from both the copyright holder and the publisher.

Published by:
Targum Press, Inc.
22700 W. Eleven Mile Rd.
Southfield, MI 48034
E-mail: targum@elronet.co.il
Fax toll free: 888-298-9992

Distributed by:
Feldheim Publishers
200 Airport Executive Park
Nanuet, NY 10954
www.feldheim.com

Printed in Israel

DEDICATION

I would like to dedicate this book
to the memory of my dear husband
Rafael ben Selim
Ralph, *zt"l*
who gave me the love of cooking.

ACKNOWLEDGMENTS

I cannot take credit for originating all of these recipes, but I have tried all of them with great satisfaction and praise. These recipes have been handed down by my family and friends throughout the years, and to all those who have contributed to this book, I extend my gratitude.

Here's hoping that you enjoy your cooking as much as I do.

Special thanks to:

Beverly Grundfast — who edited the recipes and Introduction.
Irma Charles — for encouraging me to get the book published.
Bonnie Mansour — co-editor.
Linda Dayan — co-editor.
Mozelle Tawil Mayer — photographer.

CONTENTS

Introduction 11
A Guide to Middle Eastern Products 13
Food Preparation Tips 15
APPETIZERS 17
SALADS 41
SOUPS 49
SAUCES 57
RICE 63
VEGETABLES 69
MEAT DISHES 83
CHICKEN DISHES 103
FISH 113
DAIRY DISHES 119
DESSERTS 139
   Equivalents 183
   Glossary 185
   Index 187

INTRODUCTION

One day, I received a call from my sister Renee. Someone had approached her about beginning Sephardic Syrian cooking classes at the Spanish Portuguese Synagogue in New York City. She recommended me as a possible teacher.

From the beginning of my married life, I had enjoyed cooking for my husband and family. Throughout those years I cooked and entertained extensively and now I was excited by such a challenge. I contacted the congregation and arranged to teach a class once a week for eight weeks.

This opened vistas for me. Ever since, I have been conducting cooking classes at the Beth Torah Synagogue and the Sephardic Community Center in Brooklyn. I have supervised numerous cooking demonstrations throughout the New York metropolitan area and northern New Jersey.

I was privileged to have my recipes featured at different times in the *New York Times, New York Daily News, New York Post, Kosher Gourmet Magazine,* and *The Brooklyn Cookbook.* A videotape featuring my Middle Eastern cooking recipes is currently available through Albert Dabah Video Portfolios, 142 W. 24 St., NY, NY 10011.

My greatest desire is to teach others that through the care and love that a woman puts into her meals, her table becomes the heart of the home, from which all those around it derive warmth and pleasure. I gain great satisfaction from teaching this energetic generation, who are just starting families, that cooking and serving can bring close ties among all family members.

My aim is to retain our wonderful Syrian Jewish traditions by giving my readers the recipes which have been handed down from our ancestors. Hopefully, they will be perpetuated by our descendants. Those not of Sephardic origin, too, will enjoy these delicious and sometimes exotic dishes.

My readers may be surprised to find several recipes that are not of Sephardic origin. I have several sources for my recipes, and if it was easy and tasty, I included it in my collection, regardless of its ethnic origin.

When we think about cooking or baking something new and exotic for our families and guests, the idea is pushed aside because we lack the time or know-how to make the attempt. With this book, experienced cooks and novices alike will be able to create gourmet dishes easily by following the clear step-by-step instructions.

For those on the receiving end of these marvelous dishes: Remember to show appreciation to our hard-working cooks with compliments. The added benefit is, of course, a happier cook who is always striving to be even better.

A GUIDE TO MIDDLE EASTERN PRODUCTS

Please note: There are several brands of these specialty products on the market today. Check that the one you buy has proper rabbinical supervision.

Egg roll dough

    This is a very thin quality dough that, in addition to making egg rolls, is perfect for preparing traditional Sephardic dishes. Prepared egg roll leaves can be purchased in Middle and Far Eastern specialty stores. Or, alternatively, here is a recipe to prepare your own:

    5 cups flour
    2 eggs
    ¼ tsp. salt
    2 cups cold water

    Combine first 3 ingredients in a food processor. Gradually add water until mixture forms a ball of dough. Roll out dough on a floured board, making it as thin as possible, and cut 3-inch rounds or squares.

Kanafe — Shredded dough

    Kanafe, also called Katifi, is shredded phyllo dough. This traditional dough can be purchased at stores that sell Middle Eastern products. Defrost it in the refrigerator.

Kibbe meat

This is ground beef mixed with ground rice. Kibbe meat can be purchased at butchers in neighborhoods with large Sephardic populations.

To make your own:

Grind 7 oz. uncooked rice in a spice or coffee grinder.
Add 1 lb. ground meat, and mix.

Orange water

Orange water is orange blossom water flavoring. It is used in Middle Eastern desserts and has a very distinctive and delicious flavor. It can be purchased in any Middle Eastern grocery store.

Phyllo dough

This classic dough can be found in the frozen food section of Middle Eastern stores. Today it is becoming more popular and can often be found in mainstream supermarkets as well. Let it defrost completely in the refrigerator before working with it.

Pignolia nuts

Pignolia nuts are also known as pine nuts. These are used in much Mediterranean cuisine.

Tahini

Sesame seed paste, also known as techinah. Can usually be found in mainstream supermarkets.

Tamarind

Authentic tamarind is a classic Sephardic food flavoring made from blocks of brown tamarind pods. Bottled tamarind sauce must be purchased with reliable kashrut supervision. See the recipe for a tasty substitute, Mock Tamarind Sauce, on page 62.

FOOD PREPARATION TIPS

To section oranges and grapefruits
  Remove skin and flesh with a knife. Cut segments from between walls of membrane.

To peel tomatoes and peaches
  Place tomatoes or peaches in boiling water for 30 seconds. Remove from pan and immediately place in cold water. The skin will slip off easily.

To toast nuts
  Place ½ cup nuts in ungreased heavy skillet. Cook over medium heat 5 to 7 minutes, stirring constantly until golden brown.

To clarify margarine or butter
  Bring margarine or butter to a boil, and boil for about half a minute. Cool for at least 10 minutes. Spoon out clarified margarine or butter into a bowl, and discard white residue on bottom. The clarification prevents phyllo from becoming soggy. Clarified margarine or butter may be prepared in advance, refrigerated, and melted when ready to use.

To dry fresh mint leaves

Wash leaves and remove stems. Dry leaves with paper towel. Place leaves on a fresh paper towel and let them dry for 3 to 4 days. When fully dried, crush with your fingers. Store in a closed jar.

To clean chicken

Rub the inside and outside of chicken with half a lemon and coarse salt. Rinse well.

To freeze artichoke hearts

Mix 6 cups of water, 1½ cups bottled lemon juice, and 2 Tbsps. coarse salt in a bowl. Place hearts in lemon mixture and refrigerate for 24 hours. Drain, place in plastic bag, and freeze. Will remain light in color until ready to use.

APPETIZERS

Baba Ghanouj (Eggplant and Tahini Salad)   23
Bazaghan (Cracked Wheat Salad)   20
Bestell (Meat-Filled Dough)   21
Blehat (Meat Stuffed with Egg)   19
Cheddar-Cheese Balls   24
Chicken in Phyllo   22
Eggplant Salad   25
Egg Rolls   26
Empanadas   27
Kibbe Matzah (with Fish Filling for Pesach)   30
Kibbe Neye   37
Kibbe Torpedoes   29
Kibbe with Vegetable Filling   31
Lahemageen (Meat Pizza)   32
Mushroom Turnovers   33
Pickled Cauliflower, Turnips, and Cabbage   36
Pickled Green Peppers and Carrots   35
Pickled Mushrooms and Artichokes   34
Potato Knishes in Phyllo   28
Sambousak (Cheese-and-Egg-Filled Dough)   39
Spinach Phyllo   38
Tahini Dip   40

BLEHAT
(Meat Stuffed with Egg)

Has great eye appeal. These meatballs have a surprise inside.

1 lb. ground beef
4 Tbsps. matzah meal
4 eggs
1 tsp. allspice
1 tsp. cinnamon
1 tsp. cumin
½ tsp. salt
8 oz. tomato sauce
1 cup water

Yields 6 servings.

- Mix meat, matzah meal, 1 egg, allspice, cinnamon, cumin, and salt.
- Divide meat mixture into 6 equal parts.
- Shape each part into a ball and make a hole in each with your finger.
- Hard-boil remaining 3 eggs. Cool and peel.
- Cut hard-boiled eggs in half and put each half in a hole in meat.
- Close each portion of meat around egg half.
- Bring tomato sauce and water to a boil.
- Add stuffed meatballs to sauce. Cover and simmer for 1 hour.
- When cool, cut each ball in half or slice into ½-inch slices. May be served hot or cold.

BAZAGHAN
(Cracked Wheat Salad)

A tasty as well as healthy dip for crackers or pita bread. The tamarind adds zest.

½ cup fine bulgur (cracked wheat)
3 Tbsps. oil
1 tsp. salt
½ tsp. cumin
¼ green pepper, diced
1 small onion, diced
¼ cup ground walnuts
6 Tbsps. tamarind sauce
1 Tbsp. tomato paste
crushed cayenne pepper (optional)

Yields 2 cups.

- *Wash cracked wheat in cold water, and squeeze out excess water.*
- *Add the rest of the ingredients, and mix well.*
- *Set aside for 10 minutes, and then mix well again.*
- *May be frozen.*

APPETIZERS

BESTELL
(Meat-Filled Dough)

Easy-to-make pastry filled with meat. I serve these as part of the first course on Shabbat.

Dough
2½ cups flour
½ cup semolina
1 cup margarine, room temperature
2 tsps. coarse salt
½ cup cold water
sesame seeds

Filling
2 Tbsps. oil
1 large onion, chopped
1 lb. ground beef
2 tsps. allspice
1 tsp. cinnamon
1 tsp. coarse salt
¼ cup chopped walnuts or pignolia nuts (optional)

Yields 60.

- *Mix flour and semolina in a food processor or mixer.*
- *Add margarine, and mix well.*
- *Dissolve salt in cold water and add to flour mixture, beating until mixture forms a ball of dough. Set aside.*
- *Sauté onion in oil until the onion is transparent.*
- *Add ground meat to onion, mix well, and cook uncovered on medium flame for 20 minutes, stirring occasionally. Remove from flame.*
- *Drain excess liquid from meat mixture. Add allspice, cinnamon, salt, and nuts.*
- *Shape dough into walnut-size balls.*
- *Dip one side of each ball in sesame seeds.*
- *Roll out ball, seeded side down, into a 3-inch circle (may use a tortilla press).*
- *Place 1 heaping teaspoon of meat filling in center of each circle and fold circle in half.*
- *Seal edges of half circle by pressing together or fluting with the prongs of a fork. (The bestell may be frozen at this point.)*
- *Bake on ungreased cookie sheet at 400°F for 15 to 20 minutes. If frozen, bake straight from the freezer for 25 minutes.*

CHICKEN IN PHYLLO

Phyllo is a paper-thin dough. Keep it covered with a towel when working with it to prevent it from drying it.

1 lb. chicken cutlets
2 tsp. salt
1/8 tsp. pepper
1/4 tsp. paprika
2 Tbsps. flour
4 Tbsps. oil
1 onion, chopped
12 oz. fresh mushrooms, sliced
2 Tbsps. pignolia nuts
1/4 cup chopped parsley
1 cup margarine
1 lb. phyllo dough (22 sheets of phyllo)
sesame seeds

Yields 50.

- *Cut chicken cutlets into 1/2-inch strips.*
- *Combine 2 of the teaspoons of salt with pepper, paprika, and flour.*
- *Dip chicken strips into mixture, and sauté chicken in 2 tablespoons hot oil for 3 minutes.*
- *In another saucepan, sauté onions in remaining 2 tablespoons oil until lightly browned.*
- *Add mushrooms and remaining teaspoon salt to onions.*
- *Cook onions and mushrooms until liquid evaporates. Add pignolia nuts. Cool, and add parsley.*
- *Clarify margarine (see Food Prep. Tips, p. 15). Cut phyllo sheets in half, so that each half-sheet measures 7 1/2 by 12 inches. Remove 1 sheet of phyllo, place in a vertical position, and brush with margarine on one side, using pastry brush or 2-inch paintbrush.*
- *Place a few chicken strips with 1 tablespoon onion-and-mushroom mixture at bottom of phyllo. Fold edge over filling and roll up. After 2 turns, fold the sides in and continue rolling up.*
- *Brush with margarine and sprinkle sesame seeds on top.*

(recipe continued next page)

- *Bake at 350°F for 20 minutes.*
- *Make gravy with leftover mushroom mixture by adding a 10-ounce can of clear chicken broth.*
- *May be frozen. To avoid breakage, store in a box in the freezer.*

BABA GHANOUJ
(Eggplant and Tahini Salad)

A nice change from the familiar eggplant dip, for those that like tahini.

1 medium-size eggplant, dark in color, light in weight
juice of 1 lemon
¼ cup tahini (sesame-seed paste)
1 clove garlic, crushed
1 tsp. cumin
½ tsp. coarse salt

Yields 1½ cups.

- *Split eggplant in half lengthwise.*
- *Place both halves face down on foil.*
- *Broil eggplant 3 inches from heat source for 15 to 20 minutes.*
- *Squeeze juice from lemon into a mixing bowl.*
- *When the eggplant is broiled, remove the dark, bitter seeds while still hot.*
- *Scoop out the remaining eggplant.*
- *Add eggplant to lemon juice.*
- *Add tahini, garlic, cumin, and salt, and mix well.*
- *May be frozen.*

CHEDDAR-CHEESE BALLS

The dough can also be molded into a pretzel twist. Easy to prepare and a favorite with the children.

3 cups flour
1 cup butter
8 oz. cheddar cheese, grated
1 tsp. baking powder
½ cup cold water
1 tsp. salt
sesame seeds
small pimento-stuffed olives

Yields 60.

- *Blend flour and butter in a food processor or mixer until crumbly.*
- *Add cheddar cheese and baking powder.*
- *Dissolve salt in cold water.*
- *Add salt water to flour-and-cheese mixture, beating until mixture forms a ball.*
- *Shape dough into walnut-size balls.*
- *Dip balls into sesame seeds.*
- *Make an indentation in the center of each ball and place in it an olive, pimento side up.*
- *Bake at 400°F for 20 to 30 minutes until lightly browned on bottom.*
- *May be frozen before baking. Do not defrost before baking.*

EGGPLANT SALAD

Another dish for eggplant lovers. The onion and vegetables make it especially tasty.

1 eggplant
juice of 1 lemon
¼ green pepper, chopped
1 small tomato, chopped
6 scallions, chopped
1 tsp. salt
½ tsp. cumin
dash of cayenne pepper
¼ cup chopped parsley

Yields 2 cups.

- *Split eggplant in half lengthwise.*
- *Place both halves face down on foil.*
- *Broil eggplant 3 inches from heat source for 15 to 20 minutes.*
- *When broiled, remove dark seeds. Scoop out eggplant and immediately put into lemon juice.*
- *Add green pepper, tomato, scallions, salt, cumin, cayenne pepper, and parsley, blending well.*

EGG ROLLS

Can hardly be satisfied with just one — they're great!

1 lb. chicken cutlets, cut into small pieces

2 Tbsps. oil

2 cups shredded cabbage

3 scallions including stems, chopped

1 cup chopped onion

½ cup grated carrots

10 oz. fresh mushrooms, sliced

6 oz. canned water chestnuts, sliced

2 Tbsps. soy sauce

1 tsp. salt

1 tsp. pepper

¼ tsp. sugar

1 lb. egg-roll dough or phyllo dough

1 egg white or a few drops of oil

Yields 50.

- *Sauté chicken in 2 tablespoons oil for 4 to 5 minutes.*
- *In a separate saucepan, sauté all vegetables, mushrooms, and water chestnuts for a few minutes, and place in a bowl.*
- *Add chicken, soy sauce, and spices to vegetables.*
- *If using egg-roll dough, brush the inside of each 3 by 3-inch sheet with egg white, add 2 teaspoons filling, and fold in sides and roll up. If using phyllo, divide each sheet into half-sheets, each measuring 7½ by 12 inches. Brush each half-sheet lightly with oil, add 2 teaspoons of filling, and roll up, tucking in the sides.*
- *Deep-fry until golden or bake at 400°F for 15 to 20 minutes.*
- *Egg rolls may be frozen before frying or baking. If using phyllo dough, when freezing the egg rolls, store them layered in a box with wax paper between each layer. Do not defrost before baking.*

EMPANADAS

Similar to meat kreplach but fried. Best when eaten right after frying.

2 Tbsps. oil
1 onion, chopped
1 clove garlic, minced
½ green pepper, chopped
1 lb. ground beef
¾ cup tomato sauce
2 Tbsps. vinegar
1 tsp. oregano
1 tsp. coarse salt
1 lb. egg-roll dough, 3-inch squares or rounds, or prepared ravioli dough
oil for deep frying

Yields 50.

- *Heat oil.*
- *Sauté onion, garlic, and green pepper in hot oil until translucent.*
- *Add ground meat, tomato sauce, vinegar, oregano, and salt.*
- *Cook until liquid is evaporated, about 20 minutes.*
- *Wet edge of each square or circle of egg-roll dough with a few drops of water.*
- *Fill each with 1 tablespoon of meat mixture.*
- *Fold dough in half and seal well, pressing fork around edges.*
- *Deep-fry until brown and crisp, about 1 minute.*
- *May be frozen before frying. Do not defrost before frying.*

POTATO KNISHES IN PHYLLO

A pleasant change from the traditional knish.

3 lbs. potatoes, peeled and cut in chunks
3 onions, chopped
½ cup oil
1 egg yolk
2 tsps. coarse salt
¾ tsp. pepper
2 heaping Tbsps. prepared mustard
1 cup butter or margarine
1 lb. phyllo dough
sesame seeds

Yields 50.

- *Place potatoes in pot with enough water to cover.*
- *Boil until soft, about 20 minutes.*
- *While potatoes are boiling, sauté onions in oil until golden brown.*
- *Drain and mash potatoes with a potato masher or a ricer.*
- *Add sautéed onions, egg yolk, salt, pepper, and mustard to mashed potatoes.*
- *Clarify butter or margarine (see Food Prep. Tips, p. 15).*
- *Cut phyllo sheets in half so that each half-sheet measures 7½ inches by 12 inches. Lightly brush clarified butter or margarine onto each half-sheet of phyllo with a pastry brush or 2-inch paintbrush.*
- *Fold phyllo in thirds, overlapping the longer sides of the phyllo.*
- *Brush top with butter or margarine again.*
- *Place 1 heaping teaspoon of potato mixture into corner.*
- *Fold corner into triangle shape. Continue folding in triangle fashion to end of strip.*
- *Brush tops with butter or margarine, and sprinkle sesame seeds on top.*
- *To freeze, layer unbaked knishes in a box, placing wax paper between each layer. Do not defrost before baking.*
- *Bake at 350°F for 20 minutes or until bottom is slightly browned.*

KIBBE TORPEDOES

A long, torpedo-shaped, cracked-wheat shell, filled with ground meat. I freeze lots of these and fry them before Shabbat.

Filling
3 onions, chopped
2 Tbsps. oil
3 lbs. ground shoulder steak
2 tsps. allspice
1 tsp. cinnamon
2 tsps. coarse salt
1 cup pignolia nuts

Dough
2 lbs. bulgur (fine cracked wheat)
8 oz. tomato sauce
4 Tbsps. cumin
3 Tbsps. coarse salt
6 Tbsps. oil
dash of crushed red pepper (optional)
2¼ cups flour
oil for frying

Yields 50.

- **To prepare filling:** Sauté onions in oil for 5 minutes.
- Add ground meat and mix well.
- Cook for 20 minutes, stirring occasionally.
- Drain excess liquid, and let cool.
- Add allspice, cinnamon, salt, and pignolia nuts to meat mixture.
- **To prepare dough:** Wash bulgur in cold water. Drain but do not squeeze water out of bulgur.
- Add tomato sauce, cumin, salt, oil, and red pepper to bulgur.
- Mix well, then add flour.
- Knead well.
- If it is too difficult to handle, let stand a while.
- Push dough through meat grinder with a cylinder kibbe attachment.
- As the dough slides through the cylinder, cut off 3-inch lengths.
- Dipping fingers in cold water, close one end and loosely fill with meat filling. Close other end well.
- Deep-fry until golden brown.
- May be frozen before frying, but thaw a bit first.

KIBBE MATZAH
(with Fish Filling for Pesach)

A pareve version of the meat kibbe, a real Pesach treat.

<u>Filling</u>
1 lb. flounder fillets
1 tsp. salt
flour or potato starch
1 large onion
4 Tbsps. oil
¼ cup chopped walnuts
1 tsp. cinnamon

<u>Dough</u>
2 cups matzah meal
1 cup matzah farfel
2 Tbsps. oil
4 tsps. cumin
1 tsp. paprika
½ tsp. red pepper (optional)
2 cups water
2 Tbsps. salt

Yields 30.

- ***To prepare filling:*** *Sprinkle fish with salt, and dust with flour or potato starch.*
- *Sauté fish lightly for 3 to 5 minutes on each side. Set aside to cool.*
- *When fish is cool, flake fish with a fork.*
- *Sauté onion in oil, and add nuts.*
- *Add onion-and-nut mixture and cinnamon to flaked fish.*
- ***To prepare dough:*** *Combine matzah meal, matzah farfel, oil, cumin, paprika, and red pepper.*
- *Dissolve salt in water, and slowly add salt water to mixture until dough holds together in your hand.*
- *Push dough through meat grinder with a cylinder kibbe attachment.*
- *Cut off 3-inch lengths.*
- *With wet hands, close one end of kibbe dough, and fill with fish mixture. Close other end.*
- *Deep-fry until golden brown.*

KIBBE WITH VEGETABLE FILLING

A really nutritional form of kibbe.

<u>Filling</u>
3 Tbsps. oil
1 large onion, chopped
2 cloves garlic, minced
1 medium eggplant, peeled and cubed
2 medium zucchini, cubed
1 lb. fresh mushrooms, chopped
10 oz. canned chickpeas, drained and cut in half
1 tsp. cumin
1 tsp. salt
¼ tsp. pepper
¼ tsp. crushed red pepper (optional)

Yields 50.

- *Prepare kibbe dough as directed (see dough instructions on page 29).*
- *Sauté onion and garlic in oil until transparent.*
- *Add eggplant, zucchini, and mushrooms, and mix.*
- *Add chickpeas and spices.*
- *Sauté vegetable mixture on high flame until vegetables are partially cooked, about 3 minutes.*
- *Let cool before filling dough.*
- *Deep-fry until golden brown.*

LAHEMAGEEN
(Meat Pizza)

A unique pizza-style hors d'oeuvre for a meat meal.

Dough
4½ cups flour
1 tsp. baking powder
4 Tbsps. oil
1⅓ cups cold water
2 Tbsps. coarse salt

Filling
2 lbs. ground beef
1½ cups tamarind sauce
2 Tbsps. oil
1 tsp. allspice
1 tsp. cinnamon
2 tsps. coarse salt
2 large onions, finely chopped
pignolia nuts

Yields 60.

- **To prepare dough:** *Mix flour, baking powder, and oil in a food processor.*
- *Dissolve salt in water, and add to flour mixture, beating until mixture forms a ball of dough.*
- *Knead well until dough is soft and slightly elastic, and set aside for half an hour.*
- **To prepare filling:** *Mix meat, tamarind sauce, oil, allspice, cinnamon, salt, and onions.*
- *Divide dough into 4 equal portions.*
- *Roll out one portion of dough on a floured board as thinly as possible.*
- *Using a glass cup, cut out dough into 3-inch circles and place 1 tablespoon of meat filling on each circle, pressing down meat to cover circle.*
- *Place six pignolia nuts on each circle.*
- *Repeat for remaining 3 portions of dough.*
- *Bake on a well-greased pan for 15 to 20 minutes at 400 °F until bottoms are slightly browned.*
- *May be frozen before or after baking. If frozen unbaked, do not defrost before baking.*

MUSHROOM TURNOVERS

A dairy appetizer appealing to mushroom lovers.

<u>Pastry</u>
½ cup sweet butter
4 oz. cream cheese
1½ cups flour
½ tsp. coarse salt

<u>Filling</u>
⅜ cup butter
2 cloves garlic, minced
1 lb. fresh mushrooms, sliced
⅓ cup white wine
1 tsp. coarse salt
⅛ tsp. pepper
4 Tbsps. chopped parsley
2 Tbsps. dried chives
½ cup sour cream
1 egg yolk
1 Tbsp. water

Yields 30.

- **To prepare pastry:** Mix butter and cream cheese in a mixer until smooth.
- Add flour and salt, and blend well.
- Divide dough in half, wrap each half in plastic wrap, and refrigerate for 30 minutes.
- **To prepare filling:** Sauté garlic and mushrooms in butter for 3 minutes.
- Add wine, and cook until liquid has evaporated.
- Add salt, pepper, parsley, and chives. Remove from heat, and add sour cream.
- Cool and refrigerate.
- When dough is ready, roll out each half, and using a glass cup cut into 3-inch circles.
- Fill each circle with 1 teaspoon mushroom filling, fold circle in half, and press together edges to seal.
- Mix egg yolk and water and brush on top of turnovers.
- Bake on an ungreased baking pan for 20 minutes at 400°F.
- May be frozen before baking.

PICKLED MUSHROOMS AND ARTICHOKES

An excellent accompaniment for appetizers.

1 lb. medium-size mushrooms or 8 artichokes
2 cups lemon juice
¼ cup oil
1 Tbs. coarse salt

Mushrooms:

- Cut off ends of mushroom stems, wash, and dry on a paper towel.
- Pour lemon juice into a 1-quart jar, and immediately add mushrooms to lemon juice in order for them to remain white.
- Add oil to jar and then 1 tablespoon salt.
- Seal jar well and place in refrigerator upside down. Refrigerate for 2 days before serving.
- Serve chilled or at room temperature.
- May be kept in the refrigerator for 1 month.

Artichokes:

- Remove outer, dark green leaves of artichokes, leaving the yellowish hearts.
- Cut off the top 1½ inches and discard.
- Peel stem, cut artichoke hearts in quarters, and remove fuzz.
- Pickle and store as for mushrooms.

PICKLED GREEN PEPPERS AND CARROTS

Delicious and so easy. If you've never pickled vegetables, start with these.

<u>Pickling liquid</u>
6 cups water
2 cups vinegar
4 Tbsps. coarse salt

4 green peppers
4 stalks celery
6 cloves garlic
2 lbs. carrots

Yields 12–15 servings.

Green Peppers:
- *In a bowl mix water, vinegar, and salt.*
- *Cut green peppers in slices, lengthwise.*
- *Chop 2 stalks celery in 1-inch pieces, and halve 3 cloves of garlic.*
- *Place green peppers, celery, and garlic into a 2-quart jar, and add half of the vinegar mixture.*
- *Seal tightly and immediately refrigerate. Leave in refrigerator for 2 days before serving.*
- *Keeps indefinitely in refrigerator.*

Carrots:
- *Peel and slice carrots into ½-inch diagonals.*
- *Chop 2 remaining stalks of celery into 1-inch pieces, and halve 3 remaining garlic cloves.*
- *Place carrots, celery, and garlic in a 2-quart jar, and add remaining half of the vinegar mixture.*
- *Seal jar tightly and refrigerate for 2 days. Keeps indefinitely in refrigerator.*

PICKLED CAULIFLOWER, TURNIPS, AND CABBAGE

A real child pleaser, and adults love them too. You can use boiled water to hasten the pickling process.

3 cups water
1 cup vinegar
2 Tbsps. coarse salt
4 cloves garlic, halved
1 beet, peeled and halved
1 cauliflower, cut into florets, **or**
1 medium cabbage, cut into chunks, **or**
2 lbs. small turnips, peeled and sliced into 6 slices each

Yields 12–15 servings.

- Mix together water, vinegar, and salt.
- Put vegetables into a 2-quart jar with garlic and half a beet.
- Pour vinegar mixture into jar to cover vegetables.
- Put ½ beet on top of vegetables.
- Close jar tightly, and refrigerate for 3 days.
- May be kept in refrigerator for up to 1 month.
- Each vegetable should be prepared and bottled separately.

APPETIZERS

KIBBE NEYE

This was originally a vegetarian substitute for the original kibbe that was made with raw chopped meat. This is healthier and has a taste of its own.

1 ripe tomato, chopped
1 green pepper, chopped
1 bunch parsley, chopped
½ cup red lentils
1½ cups water
3 onions, chopped
2 Tbsps. oil
1¼ cups fine bulgur (cracked wheat)
3 oz. tomato paste
3 Tbsps. ketchup
1 Tbsp. cumin
1 Tbsp. coarse salt
a few grains of crushed red pepper (optional)

Yields 30.

- *Remove all excess liquid from chopped tomatoes, green pepper, and parsley, and wrap in a paper towel.*
- *Clean red lentils, removing small stones.*
- *Wash lentils well. Drain.*
- *Boil lentils in 1½ cups water. Simmer, covered, for 20 minutes.*
- *Sauté onions in oil until transparent.*
- *Wash bulgur in cold water, and drain, squeezing out excess liquid.*
- *Add tomatoes, green pepper, parsley, hot lentils, and onions to bulgur, and mix well.*
- *Add tomato paste, ketchup, cumin, and salt, and mix.*
- *Form into 2-inch-long torpedo shapes, and serve.*
- *Should not be frozen.*

SPINACH PHYLLO

This recipe takes time but is surely worth the effort. For an easier version, it can be made without the phyllo in a casserole dish.

1 lb. phyllo dough
20 oz. frozen chopped spinach
2 Tbsps. oil
1 large onion, chopped
3 eggs
½ lb. muenster cheese, grated
1 tsp. salt
½ tsp. pepper
1 cup sweet butter, clarified
sesame seeds

Yields 60.

- Cut phyllo sheets in half so that each half-sheet measures 7½ by 12 inches. Cover sheets well with a dish towel, and refrigerate until ready to use.
- Defrost spinach, and squeeze out all excess liquid.
- Sauté onion in oil until transparent.
- Beat eggs, then add spinach, onion, cheese, salt, pepper, and 2 tablespoons melted butter.
- Clarify butter (see Food Prep. Tips, p. 15).
- Remove 1 half-sheet of phyllo and brush gently with butter, using a pastry brush or 2-inch paintbrush.
- Fold half-sheet of phyllo in three, lengthwise. Brush with butter again.
- Put 1 teaspoon spinach mixture in corner of phyllo strip, and fold into a triangle. Continue folding strip in triangle fashion until the end.
- Brush top with butter and sprinkle with sesame seeds. Repeat entire process for remaining half-sheets of phyllo dough.
- May be frozen at this point. To freeze, place spinach triangles in a box with wax paper between layers. Do not thaw before baking.
- Bake at 400°F for 15 to 20 minutes.

SAMBOUSAK
(Cheese-and-Egg-Filled Dough)

Picture a mini-quiche. Bet you can't eat just one!

Dough
3 cups unbleached flour
1 cup sweet butter, room temperature
½ cup cold water
2 tsps. coarse salt
sesame seeds

Filling
1½ lbs. Muenster cheese, grated
3 eggs, slightly beaten
1 tsp. baking powder
1 tsp. coarse salt
Yields 60.

- *Beat flour and butter together well in a mixer or food processor.*
- *Dissolve salt in cold water, and add to flour mixture, beating until mixture forms a ball of dough. Set aside.*
- *Mix together cheese, eggs, baking powder, and salt, blending well.*
- *Shape dough into walnut-size balls.*
- *Dip only one side of each ball into sesame seeds.*
- *Roll out each ball, seeded side down, into a 3-inch circle (may use a tortilla press).*
- *Place 1 heaping teaspoon of cheese filling in center of each circle, and fold circle in half.*
- *Seal edges of half circle by pressing together with fingers or fluting with the prongs of a fork.*
- *May be frozen at this point.*
- *Bake on an ungreased cookie sheet at 400°F for about 20 minutes, until lightly browned on bottom. If frozen, bake for 25 minutes. Do not defrost before baking.*

TAHINI DIP

I remember this from my childhood, and it was Dad's favorite. Great with pita bread or challah.

1 cup tahini (sesame seed paste)
juice of 3 lemons
½ cup water
1 tsp. cumin
2 cloves garlic, crushed
½ teaspoon salt

Yields 1½ cups.

- *Purée all ingredients together in a food processor.*

SALADS

Caesar Salad   43
Fava Bean Salad   43
Orzo Salad   44
Red Skin Potato Salad   45
Salata (Chopped Syrian Salad)   48
Tabouli (Cracked Wheat with Vegetables)   47
Tomato and Chickpea Salad   46
Whitefish Salad   48

CAESAR SALAD

A standard salad that is still popular.

1 head romaine lettuce
6 Tbsps. olive oil
3 Tbsps. wine vinegar
¼ teaspoon dry mustard
½ can anchovies
1 egg, cooked 1½ minutes (optional)
¾ cup croutons

Yields 4–5 servings.

- *Wash and clean lettuce, and tear into bite-size pieces.*
- *Mix olive oil, vinegar, mustard, anchovies, and egg, and pour over lettuce just before serving.*
- *Sprinkle croutons on top.*

FAVA BEAN SALAD

This is a bean lover's favorite.

24 oz. cooked fava beans
1 bunch scallions, bulbs and stems sliced
1 bunch parsley, chopped
juice of 3 lemons
2 Tbsps. oil
2 cloves garlic, minced
1 tsp. coarse salt
2 tsps. cumin
¼ tsp. crushed red pepper (optional)

Yields 4 cups.

- *Rinse and drain beans.*
- *Add scallions, parsley, lemon juice, oil, garlic, salt, cumin, and red pepper to beans.*
- *Refrigerate for half an hour. Serve chilled.*
- *Keeps for 2 to 3 days in refrigerator.*

ORZO SALAD

A colorful change from your ordinary pasta salad. Orzo is a rice-shaped pasta. However, any pasta may be used.

16 oz. pkg. orzo

½ cup Italian salad dressing

3 cloves garlic, chopped

10 oz. fresh mushrooms, sliced

4 large carrots, sliced

1 bunch broccoli florets, cut into bite-size chunks

½ cup olive oil

2 Tbsps. soy sauce

½ tsp. salt

½ tsp. sugar

½ cup parsley, chopped

¼ cup apple cider vinegar

Yields 6–8 servings.

- *Cook orzo in a 3-quart saucepan according to package instructions. Drain, and add Italian dressing.*
- *Sauté garlic and sliced mushrooms until golden brown.*
- *Boil carrots and broccoli for 10 minutes.*
- *Mix olive oil, soy sauce, salt, sugar, parsley, and vinegar.*
- *Add all ingredients to orzo mixture.*
- *Chill for 20 minutes, and serve.*

RED SKIN POTATO SALAD

Who doesn't love potato salad? Especially this one.

2 lbs. small red skin potatoes

4 hard-boiled eggs, diced

½ dill pickle, diced

½ onion, chopped

¼ cup chopped celery

2 oz. sliced pimentos

½ cup mayonnaise

2 Tbsps. prepared mustard

2 Tbsps. tarragon vinegar

¼ tsp. salt

⅛ tsp. pepper

Yields 6–8 servings.

- *Wash potatoes well, and boil for 30 minutes or until tender.*
- *Drain and cool completely.*
- *Cut potatoes into cubes and add all other ingredients.*

TOMATO AND CHICKPEA SALAD

A nice change from the usual green salad.

4 medium tomatoes, peeled (see p. 15), seeded, and chopped

1½ cups chopped celery

2 small cucumbers, peeled, seeded, and chopped

1 green pepper, chopped

1 red pepper, chopped

1 large onion, chopped

16 oz. canned chickpeas

<u>Dressing</u>

½ cup red wine vinegar

1 cup oil

1 Tbsp. Dijon mustard

2 cloves garlic, crushed

¼ cup chopped dill

2 tsp. salt

½ tsp. pepper

Yields 6–8 servings.

- Combine tomatoes, celery, cucumbers, peppers, onion, and chickpeas.
- Combine all the dressing ingredients, using a whisk or a blender.
- Add salad dressing to the vegetables, and mix well.
- Marinate in refrigerator for at least two hours before serving.

TABOULI
(Cracked Wheat with Vegetables)

Vegetarians love this cracked wheat salad.

½ cup fine bulgur (cracked wheat)

1 cup warm water

2 Tbsps. oil

1 tsp. salt

1 tsp. dried mint (see Food Prep. Tips, p. 16)

1 tsp. cumin

1 bunch scallions, diced

1 bunch parsley, chopped

2 tomatoes, diced

2 small cucumbers, diced

juice of 2 lemons

a few grains of crushed red pepper

Yields 4–6 servings.

- Soak bulgur in warm water for half an hour.
- Drain, squeezing out excess water.
- Add remaining ingredients, and mix well.
- Marinate in refrigerator for at least 2 hours before serving. Serve chilled.

SALATA
(Chopped Syrian Salad)

Especially good with barbecued poultry and meat.

2 cucumbers, diced
2 tomatoes, diced
6 scallions, sliced
½ cup chopped parsley
1 Tbsp. oil
½ tsp. coarse salt
½ tsp. cumin
juice of 1 to 2 lemons

Yields 4 servings.

- *Mix all ingredients together.*
- *Refrigerate for half an hour before serving.*

WHITEFISH SALAD

Different from the usual tuna salad. Be careful when boning the smoked whitefish.

3 lbs. smoked whitefish
2 Tbsps. mayonnaise
½ small onion, chopped
1 stalk celery, chopped
juice of 1 lemon
1 tsp. salt
cucumbers, thinly sliced

Yields 6–8 servings.

- *Fillet and flake fish.*
- *Add mayonnaise, onion, celery, lemon juice, and salt, and mix gently.*
- *Top with cucumber slices, and serve.*

SOUPS

Ades (Red Lentil Soup)   52
Chicken Soup   51
Gazpacho   56
Lentil-Noodle Soup   52
Matzah Balls   55
Onion Soup   54
Shurba (Rice Soup with Kibbe)   55
Split Pea Soup with Chicken   53

CHICKEN SOUP

When I first got married my husband requested chicken soup, and I heartily agreed to make it. When we were ready to eat, I asked him to come and help me strain it. Without thinking, we held the strainer over the sink and poured all the soup into the strainer with the soup going down the drain. This should be proof that all beginners can become cooks.

1 chicken
6 cups water
2 onions
3 stalks celery, cut into large chunks
2 carrots
2 tsps. salt
optional: 1 bay leaf or 1 bunch of dill

Yields 6 servings.

- *Clean chicken and rub with salt.*
- *Put chicken in pot of water with onions, celery, carrots, and salt.*
- *Bring to a boil, cover, and simmer for 1 hour.*
- *Optional: The soup can be strained at this point. Remove chicken and vegetables before straining.*
- *Cut up and bone chicken, and add cut up chicken to soup.*

LENTIL-NOODLE SOUP

This recipe is perfect for a cold winter night. It's quick to prepare and very filling.

1 large onion, chopped
2 Tbsps. oil
6 cups water
¾ cup lentils
1 Tbsp. salt
⅛ tsp. pepper
½ lb. medium noodles

Yields 6 servings.

- *Sauté onion in oil.*
- *Add water to sautéed onions and bring to a boil.*
- *Check and wash lentils, and add lentils, salt, and pepper to water.*
- *Cook for approximately 20 minutes, or until done.*
- *Add noodles, simmer for about 15 minutes, and serve immediately.*

ADES
(Red Lentil Soup)

This soup is a very authentic part of our Sephardic tradition. The spices add to the unique flavor of the lentils.

1 cup red lentils
4 cups water
2 cloves garlic, crushed
1 tsp. coarse salt
¼ tsp. coriander
2 Tbsps. oil
¼ tsp. cumin

Yields 3–4 servings.

- *Wash and check lentils and remove stones.*
- *Bring water to boil, and add lentils.*
- *Bring water to a boil again, and simmer for 20 minutes.*
- *Make a paste of garlic, salt, and coriander.*
- *Fry garlic in oil until golden brown, and add to lentil mixture.*
- *Cover and simmer for 1 hour.*
- *Before serving, add cumin. Serve with lemon wedges and toasted pita bread.*

SPLIT PEA SOUP WITH CHICKEN

This is a dish that makes an all-in-one meal.

3 to 4-lb. chicken
5 cups water
2 stalks celery cut into pieces
2 carrots, halved
1 onion, cut into fourths
1 cup split peas
1 cup diced celery
1 cup diced carrots
1 cup diced potatoes
1 onion, chopped
2 cloves garlic
1 Tbsp. oil
1 tsp. salt
1 tsp. cumin
1 tsp. oregano
$\frac{1}{8}$ tsp. pepper

Yields 6 servings.

- *Clean chicken (see Food Prep. Tips, p. 16).*
- *Cook chicken, celery, carrots, and onion chunks in water for 15 minutes.*
- *Add split peas to soup. Cook covered for 1 hour.*
- *Remove celery, carrots, and onion from soup, and add diced celery, carrots, and potatoes.*
- *Sauté chopped onion and garlic in oil, and add to soup.*
- *Season with salt, cumin, oregano, and pepper, and cook for an additional 10 to 15 minutes.*
- *Remove chicken. Discard skin and bones. Cut chicken into pieces and return to soup.*

ONION SOUP

People may consider onions a lowly vegetable, but they sure make a great soup.

1 lb. onions, thinly sliced
1 Tbsp. oil
2 Tbsps. butter or margarine
½ tsp. salt
1 Tbsp. flour
⅛ tsp. pepper
4 cups water
4 packets vegetable broth

optional
French bread, sliced
olive oil
garlic, crushed
Parmesan cheese

Yields 3–4 servings.

- *Sauté onions in oil and margarine, together with salt, for 20 minutes until golden brown.*
- *Add flour, stir, and cook for 2 to 3 minutes.*
- *In a separate saucepan, dissolve vegetable broth powder in water, bring to a boil, and stir into onion mixture.*
- *Cover, bring to a boil, and simmer for 30 to 40 minutes.*
- *Skim off extra fat.*
- **To prepare bread:** *Brush bread slices with a little oil and crushed garlic.*
- *Bake at 400°F for about 12 minutes or until golden brown.*
- *Sprinkle with Parmesan cheese.*
- *Place in a bowl and pour soup on top.*

SHURBA
(Rice Soup with Kibbe)

This is the king of soups. As a child, I gobbled it up.

6 cups water
¾ cup rice
4 oz. tomato sauce
1 cup diced celery
1 Tbsp. salt
10 oz. canned chickpeas
12 medium kibbe (see recipe for Kibbe Balls, p. 61)

Yields 6 servings.

- *Mix water, rice, tomato sauce, celery, and salt, and bring to a boil. Simmer for approximately 20 minutes.*
- *Add chickpeas and kibbe, and cook for about 20 minutes.*
- *Serve with fresh lemon.*

MATZAH BALLS

Light and delicious. Add them to your chicken soup.

2 eggs
salt and pepper to taste
½ cup matzah meal
½ heaping tsp. baking powder

- *Beat eggs together with salt and pepper.*
- *Gradually stir in matzah meal and baking powder to egg mixture. Refrigerate for about 20 minutes.*
- *Form matzah meal mixture into balls, and add to boiling water. Cover and simmer for 45 minutes.*
- *Remove matzah balls from water and add to soup.*

GAZPACHO

The vegetables in this soup are very nutritious. Easy to make and refreshing for a summer meal.

3 small cucumbers, peeled and coarsely chopped

6 medium tomatoes, peeled (see Food Prep. Tips, p. 15) and diced

1 onion, diced

1 green pepper, diced

1 clove garlic, crushed

5½ cups cold water

½ cup wine vinegar

2 tsps. salt

5 Tbsps. olive oil

2 Tbsps. tomato paste

croutons

Yields 5–6 servings.

- *In a deep bowl, mix cucumbers, tomatoes, onion, green pepper, and garlic.*
- *Add water, vinegar, and salt, place mixture in a food processor, and blend for 1 minute.*
- *Return to bowl, add olive oil and tomato paste, and blend well.*
- *Cover bowl tightly and refrigerate for 2 hours.*
- *Just before serving, stir soup well, and garnish with croutons.*

SAUCES

Bedab Lemuna (Lemon Sauce)   62
Fresh Basil Sauce (for Pasta)   60
Keftes (Syrian Meatball Sauce)   59
Kibbe Balls (Meatballs)   61
Kibbe Homda Sauce   60
Mock Tamarind Sauce   62

KEFTES
(Syrian Meatball Sauce)

A basic sauce used often on rice.

<u>Meatballs</u>
1 lb. ground beef
1 tsp. salt
4 Tbsps. matzah meal
4 Tbsps. parsley
1 egg
2 Tbsps. oil
2 Tbsps. chopped walnuts

<u>Sauce</u>
8 oz. tomato sauce
½ cup water
juice of 1 lemon
1 tsp. salt
1 tsp. sugar

Yields about 4 cups.

- *Combine ground beef, salt, matzah meal, parsley, egg, oil, and walnuts.*
- *Shape mixture into walnut-size balls.*
- *Mix tomato sauce, water, lemon juice, salt, and sugar.*
- *Bring sauce mixture to a boil, add meatballs, and simmer for 45 minutes.*

FRESH BASIL SAUCE
(for Pasta)

A nice change from the usual tomato flavored sauces.

½ cup pignolia nuts
2 cups fresh basil leaves
4 cloves garlic
½ tsp. salt
½ tsp. pepper
⅓ cup olive oil

Yields ½ to ¾ cup.

- *On an ungreased baking pan, toast pignolia nuts at 350°F for 8 to 10 minutes.*
- *Wash and dry basil.*
- *In a food processor, mix nuts, basil, garlic, salt, and pepper.*
- *Slowly add olive oil to mixture until it forms a paste.*
- *May be frozen until ready to use.*

KIBBE HOMDA SAUCE

A traditional sauce served over rice on Friday night. Even the littlest of my grandchildren go for the lemon and mint combination.

4 cups water
1 large potato, diced
3 stalks celery, diced
1 carrot, sliced
2 cloves garlic, minced
2 tsps. dried mint (see Food Prep. Tips, p. 16).
1 tsp. salt
juice of 2 lemons

Yields 8 cups.

- *Mix together all ingredients, bring to a boil, and simmer for 20 minutes.*
- *Add kibbe balls (for recipe, see p. 61), bring sauce to a boil, and let simmer for 20 more minutes.*
- *Serve hot over rice.*

KIBBE BALLS
(Meatballs)

Kibbe Balls give vegetables a distinctive flavor. A very traditional dish.

Shell
1 lb. kibbe meat (ground beef and fine rice, see p. 14)

Filling
½ lb. ground beef
2 stalks celery, finely chopped
½ tsp. allspice
½ tsp. salt
½ tsp. cinnamon
½ Tbsp. oil

- *Make ¾-inch diameter balls with kibbe meat.*
- *Mix together ground beef, celery, allspice, salt, cinnamon, and oil.*
- *With your finger, hollow out each ball until walls are very thin. Dip your finger in water to prevent shell from sticking.*
- *Add about ½ teaspoon of filling to cavity of each ball. Close up ball by firmly pinching it together.*
- *The kibbe balls can be cooked with vegetables like peas, artichokes, or mushrooms. Brown the kibbe balls and add the vegetables with about ½ cup of water and spices. If using peas add allspice and salt; if using artichokes, season with lemon, salt, and white pepper; if adding mushrooms season with salt and pepper. Cook for about 1 hour.*
- *May be frozen until ready to use.*

BEDAB LEMUNA
(Lemon Sauce)

One of my favorite sauces while growing up. Using some of your already cooked Friday night chicken soup makes this really quick to prepare.

10 oz. clear chicken broth
2 eggs
juice of 1 lemon
1 tsp. salt
1 Tbsp. flour
1 Tbsp. water

Yields 2 cups.

- Mix chicken broth, eggs, lemon juice, and salt in a saucepan with a hand mixer or whisk.
- Dissolve flour in water, and add to sauce mixture.
- Bring sauce to a boil, stirring constantly until it thickens. If sauce is lumpy, strain.
- Cool to room temperature, and serve over rice.

MOCK TAMARIND SAUCE

Use this sauce for special flavoring for Lahemageen (see p. 32) and for vegetables.

4 cups prune juice
4 cups cranberry juice
20 oz. applesauce
17 oz. prune butter
16 oz. apricot butter
$\frac{2}{3}$ of a 1 qt. bottle of lemon juice

Yields 8 cups.

- Mix all ingredients in a large pot, and bring to a boil.
- Continue boiling until sauce thickens, about 2 hours.
- Let sauce cool completely, and store in a bottle in refrigerator for up to 6 months.

RICE

Fried Rice   66
M'gedrah (Lentils and Rice)   67
Rice, Plain or with Orzo   65
Rice with Chickpeas   66
Rice with Nuts   65
Rice with Peas   68
Spanish Rice   68

RICE, PLAIN OR WITH ORZO

Follow the instructions and say goodbye to undercooked and mushy rice. Your guests will ask you the secret. It's simple.

2 Tbsps. orzo (pasta) (optional)
2 Tbsps. oil
2 cups water
1 Tbsp. salt
1 cup rice*

Yields 3 to 4 servings.

- Bring water, oil, and salt to a boil.
- (For rice with orzo, lightly brown orzo in oil. Add water and salt to orzo, and bring water to a boil.)
- Wash rice in warm water and rinse twice.
- Drain rice and add to boiling water.
- Bring mixture to a boil again, mix well, cover, and simmer for 30 minutes.

* For 2 cups of rice use 3½ cups of water.
* For 3 cups of rice use 5 cups of water.
* For 4 cups of rice use 6½ cups of water.

RICE WITH NUTS

A special dish for special occasions.

1 onion, diced
4 Tbsps. oil
3½ cups water
2 cups rice
½ cup soy sauce
1 cup mixture of chopped peanuts, walnuts, and toasted almonds.

Yields 6–8 servings.

- Sauté onion in oil until transparent.
- Add water to sautéed onions, and bring to a boil. Add rice and soy sauce to water.
- Bring mixture to a boil again, mix well, cover, and simmer for 40 minutes.
- Serve topped with nuts.

RICE WITH CHICKPEAS

For all rice lovers, here's a great one to try.

2 cloves garlic, crushed
2 onions, chopped
2 Tbsps. oil
3½ cups water
1½ Tbsps. coarse salt
2 cups rice
10 oz. canned chickpeas
2 Tbsps. butter or margarine

- Sauté garlic and onions in oil.
- Add water and salt and bring to a boil.
- Add rice and chickpeas to onion mixture, and bring to a boil again.
- Stir well, cover, and simmer for 30 minutes.
- Add butter or margarine.

Yields 6–8 servings.

FRIED RICE

Given to me by a kosher caterer who was known for his delicious, non-greasy fried rice.

1 clove garlic, crushed
1 onion, chopped
2 Tbsps. oil
1 cup rice
2 Tbsps. soy sauce
2 packets vegetable broth powder
2 cups water

- Sauté garlic and onion in oil.
- Add rice to onion mixture, and brown.
- Add soy sauce, vegetable broth powder, and water, and bring to a boil.
- Stir well, cover, and simmer for 30 minutes.

Yields 3–4 servings.

M'GEDRAH
(Lentils and Rice)

Once a poor man's dish in Aleppo, it is now a favorite of many. Recommended as a high fiber food.

1 cup lentils
5 cups water
2 Tbsps. coarse salt
2 cups rice
3 Tbsps. butter or margarine
2 large onions, sliced
⅓ cup oil

Yields 8 servings.

- Check and rinse lentils.
- In a saucepan, combine lentils and 2 cups water.
- Cover, bring to a boil, and simmer for 15 minutes.
- Add the remaining 3 cups of water, add salt, and bring to a boil again.
- Wash rice, drain, and add to lentils. Cover and simmer for 30 minutes.
- When water is absorbed, dot rice with butter or margarine.
- In a separate pan, sauté onions in oil until brown. Sprinkle over rice and lentils.
- Serve with yogurt.

RICE WITH PEAS

This rice dish originated in the Mediterranean region.

2 cloves garlic, minced
4 Tbsps. oil
2 cups rice
2 Tbsps. salt
½ tsp. allspice
1 tsp. coriander
3½ cups water
10 oz. frozen peas

Yields 6–8 servings.

- *Brown garlic in oil.*
- *Add rice to garlic, and sauté until lightly browned.*
- *Add salt, allspice, and coriander, and mix well. Add water and peas.*
- *Bring mixture to a boil, stir, reduce flame, and simmer, covered, for 30 minutes.*

SPANISH RICE

Serve your vegetables and starch in one luscious dish.

1 onion, chopped
2 cloves garlic, minced
2 Tbsps. oil
¼ green pepper, chopped
½ lb. fresh mushrooms
3 oz. jar pimentos, sliced
¾ cup water
½ cup tomato sauce
¾ cup frozen peas
1 Tbsp. coarse salt
½ tsp. cumin
1 cup rice

Yields 4 servings.

- *Sauté onion and garlic in oil until transparent.*
- *Add green pepper, sliced mushrooms, and pimentos, and sauté for 5 minutes.*
- *Add water, tomato sauce, peas, salt, and cumin, and bring mixture to a boil.*
- *Add rice, stir, and bring to a boil again.*
- *Stir again, cover, and simmer for 30 minutes.*

VEGETABLES

Artichoke Medias (Stuffed Artichoke Hearts)   71
Artichokes in Oil   72
Asparagus Winter   72
Baked Carrots   73
Baked Fried Potatoes   80
Carrot Ring   74
Corn-Stuffed Tomatoes   81
Creamed Cauliflower and Broccoli   75
Great Northern Beans   73
Green Beans and Veal   78
Green Beans with Egg   78
Krefsiah (Swiss Chard)   82
Lubyeh (Black-Eyed Peas)   76
Ratatouille on Toast   77
Roast Potatoes   80
Stuffed Mushrooms   79
Tomato and Egg   82

VEGETABLES

ARTICHOKE MEDIAS
(Stuffed Artichoke Hearts)

A very exotic food for artichoke lovers.

6 fresh artichokes

Marinade
½ cup lemon juice
1½ cups water
1 tsp. salt

Filling
½ lb. ground beef
1 egg
½ tsp. allspice
½ tsp. cinnamon
½ tsp. cumin
3 Tbsps. matzah meal
1 tsp. coarse salt
3 Tbsps. chopped parsley

Sauce
8 oz. tomato sauce
1 cup water
1 tsp. salt
1 tsp. sugar
juice of 1 lemon
1 Tbsp. tamarind (optional)

Yields 6 servings.

- *Remove tough outer leaves from each artichoke.*
- *Cut down 1½ inches from top.*
- *Cut each artichoke heart in half and remove fuzz. (Hearts can be frozen at this point — see Food Prep. Tips, p. 16.)*
- *Combine marinade ingredients.*
- *Immediately place halved artichoke hearts in marinade, and set aside.*
- *Combine filling ingredients.*
- *Drain and dry artichoke hearts.*
- *Fill hearts with meat mixture, and fry in oil, meat side down for about 2 minutes, until meat is browned. Place hearts in casserole, meat side up.*
- *Combine sauce ingredients.*
- *Pour sauce over stuffed artichokes, and bake covered at 350°F for 40 minutes, basting often.*

ARTICHOKES IN OIL

Another way of preparing the ever popular artichoke. An unusual tasty treat.

6 artichokes
2 Tbsps. oil
1½ cups water
1 tsp. salt
juice of 2 lemons

Yields 4–6 servings.

- Remove outer leaves from artichokes, and cut off tops about 2 inches down. (If the artichokes are large, cut 3 inches down.)
- Cut each heart in half and remove fuzz.
- Immediately place hearts in lemon juice to keep them from turning brown, then drain.
- Put artichoke hearts in a saucepan, and add oil, water, salt, and lemon juice.
- Boil for about 20 minutes, or until tender.
- Serve hot or at room temperature.

ASPARAGUS WINTER

An easy and delicious way to prepare asparagus.

1 lb. fresh asparagus
salt and pepper to taste
2 Tbsps. butter or margarine

<u>Hollandaise Sauce</u>
1 cup sour cream
juice of 2 lemons
4 egg yolks
¼ tsp. paprika
1 tsp. salt

Yields 3–4 servings.

- Wash and peel asparagus and arrange in a shallow ovenproof dish.
- Sprinkle salt and pepper on asparagus, and dot with butter or margarine.
- Cover and bake at 350°F for 30 minutes.
- Combine sauce ingredients, and bring mixture to a boil, stirring constantly, until it thickens.
- Serve sauce over asparagus or on the side.

GREAT NORTHERN BEANS

A chef from South America is responsible for the flavor of these beans. Served over rice, it's a complete protein.

16 oz. dried white beans
1 large onion, chopped
2 cloves garlic, minced
2 Tbsps. oil
5 cups water
8 oz. tomato sauce
2 tsp. cumin
1½ tsps. oregano
1 Tbsp. coarse salt
½ tsp. black pepper

Yields 6–8 servings.

- *Soak beans overnight or at least 1 hour before cooking. Drain.*
- *Sauté onion and garlic in oil.*
- *Add water, drained beans, tomato sauce, cumin, oregano, salt, and pepper to onion mixture.*
- *Bring ingredients to a boil, cover, and simmer for 2 hours.*
- *Serve over rice.*

BAKED CARROTS

The sweetness of the carrots is enhanced through the baking.

1 lb. carrots
¼ cup oil or melted margarine
½ cup flavored bread crumbs

Yields 2–3 servings.

- *Peel and wash carrots.*
- *Brush each carrot with oil or margarine, and dip in bread crumbs.*
- *Place breaded carrots in a small casserole, cover, and bake at 350°F for 45 minutes or until fork-tender.*

CARROT RING

Great as a side dish with your favorite entrée but is a treat by itself as well.

1 cup margarine or solid shortening
1 cup brown sugar
2 eggs
2 Tbsps. water
4 cups grated carrots
2½ cups flour
1 tsp. salt
2 tsps. baking powder
1 tsp. cinnamon

Yields 8–10 servings.

- *Cream thoroughly shortening, sugar, eggs, and water. Add grated carrots.*
- *Mix dry ingredients, and add to carrot mixture. Mix well.*
- *Grease a 2- or 3-quart tube pan, and pour batter into pan.*
- *Place tube pan in another pan filled with 1 inch of hot water, and bake at 350°F for 1 hour, or until done.*

VEGETABLES

CREAMED CAULIFLOWER AND BROCCOLI

Make sure to use the insect-free variety. Not only for vegetable lovers.

½ head cauliflower florets
½ bunch broccoli florets

<u>Cream sauce</u>
2 Tbsps. butter
2 Tbsps. flour
1 cup milk
1 tsp. salt
¼ tsp. white pepper
3 oz. cream cheese
½ cup grated Muenster cheese
flavored bread crumbs

Yields 8 servings.

- *Steam cauliflower and broccoli for 6 minutes.*
- *Melt butter. Add flour and stir until dissolved.*
- *Add milk, salt, and pepper to butter mixture, and bring to a boil.*
- *Add cream cheese and Muenster cheese, and stir until well blended.*
- *Arrange cauliflower and broccoli in a 2-quart casserole.*
- *Add cream sauce, and sprinkle with bread crumbs.*
- *Bake for 20 minutes at 400°F.*

LUBYEH
(Black-Eyed Peas)

Used mainly for Rosh Hashanah. The family then reminds me to make it during the year as well.

1 onion, chopped
2 cloves garlic, minced
1 Tbsp. oil
½ lb. veal stew meat, cut into 1-inch cubes
1 cup water
16 oz. frozen black-eyed peas
2 tsps. salt
⅛ tsp. pepper
1 tsp. allspice
½ tsp. cinnamon
1 Tbsp. tomato paste

Yields 6 servings.

- *Lightly sauté onion and garlic in oil.*
- *Add cubed veal and half of the water to onion mixture. Cover and simmer for 20 minutes.*
- *Add black-eyed peas, salt, pepper, allspice, cinnamon, and tomato paste to veal, and combine.*
- *Add remaining ½ cup of water to mixture.*
- *Cover and cook over low heat for 1 hour. If mixture dries out, add more water.*
- *Serve hot.*

RATATOUILLE ON TOAST

Use it as an unusual appetizer or as a vegetable dish as well.

1 cup onions, diced
1 Tbsp. minced garlic
1 green pepper, diced
1 red pepper, diced
½ cup olive oil
4 cups cubed eggplant
4 cups cubed zucchini
2 large tomatoes, cubed
3 Tbsps. tomato paste
1 bay leaf
½ tsp. thyme
1 tsp. salt
¼ tsp. pepper
4 medium-size pita breads
Parmesan cheese for sprinkling

Yields 25 servings.

- *Sauté onion, garlic, and peppers in oil for 5 minutes.*
- *Add eggplant, zucchini, tomatoes, tomato paste, bay leaf, thyme, salt, and pepper.*
- *Lower flame, cover, and simmer for 20 minutes.*
- *Remove bay leaf, and drain any excess liquid from mixture. Let cool.*
- *Cut each pita into 12 wedges. Place wedges on a greased baking sheet.*
- *Place 1 tablespoon of vegetable mixture on each wedge.*
- *Sprinkle with Parmesan cheese, and bake at 350°F for 15 minutes.*

GREEN BEANS WITH EGG

My mother is the originator of this dish. It's worth passing down to the next generation.

1 lb. green beans
1 clove garlic, minced
1 Tbsp. oil
½ cup water
1 tsp. salt
1 egg, slightly beaten

Yields 3–4 servings.

- Wash green beans and cut into 1-inch pieces, removing ends.
- Sauté garlic in oil.
- Add beans, water, and salt to garlic and oil.
- Cover and steam for 30 minutes.
- Just before serving, add beaten egg to beans, stirring until egg hardens.

GREEN BEANS AND VEAL

Delicious served with rice.

2 cloves garlic, minced
2 Tbsps. oil
½ lb. shoulder veal, cubed
1½ cups water
2 lbs. green beans, ends trimmed
1 tsp. allspice
1 tsp. cinnamon
1 tsp. coarse salt

Yields 6–8 servings.

- In a saucepan, sauté garlic in oil.
- Add cubed veal, and brown.
- Add 1 cup of the water, and simmer for 30 minutes until veal is tender.
- Add green beans, allspice, cinnamon, salt, and the remaining half cup of water.
- Cover and simmer for 1 hour.

STUFFED MUSHROOMS

Mushrooms are one of the most versatile vegetables. If you find the time, try them this way.

1 lb. large mushrooms
1 onion, chopped
2 cloves garlic, minced
4 Tbsps. flavored bread crumbs
1 tsp. salt
$\frac{1}{8}$ tsp. pepper
2 Tbsps. melted margarine
3 Tbsps. oil

Yields 12 servings.

- *Wash mushrooms and remove stems.*
- *Scrape out gills from underside of mushroom caps. Rinse and dry mushroom caps on a paper towel.*
- *Chop mushroom stems, and combine with onions, garlic, bread crumbs, salt, pepper, and margarine.*
- *Fill each mushroom cap with the mushroom-onion mixture, and place on an oiled baking pan.*
- *Sprinkle the 3 tablespoons of oil over mushrooms, and bake at 425°F for 20 minutes.*
- *Can be frozen after baking.*

BAKED FRIED POTATOES

The pleasure of french fries without the guilt.

6 medium-size potatoes
½ cup water
1 Tbsp. coarse salt
½ tsp. pepper
1 tsp. paprika
2 Tbsps. margarine

Yields 6 servings.

- *Peel potatoes, and slice as for french fries.*
- *Place potatoes in a 17- by 12-inch metal baking pan, making sure they don't overlap.*
- *Cover potatoes with water, and sprinkle with salt, pepper, and paprika. Dot with margarine.*
- *Bring potatoes to a boil on top of stove.*
- *Remove pan from stove top, and bake at 400°F for 30 to 40 minutes, until golden brown.*

ROAST POTATOES

May be prepared earlier, which makes it particularly convenient when you're having company.

6 large red-skin potatoes (if not available, regular potatoes may be used)
2 medium onions, chopped
2 Tbsps. oil
2 tsps. coarse salt
¼ tsp. pepper
½ tsp. paprika
½ tsp. cinnamon

Yields 8 servings.

- *Wash and scrub potatoes with a vegetable brush.*
- *Put potatoes in a saucepan, cover with water, and bring to a boil.*
- *Simmer for 20 minutes, drain, and cool.*
- *Cut cooled potatoes into cubes.*
- *Sauté onions in oil, and then add the onions, salt, pepper, paprika, and cinnamon to the cubed potatoes.*
- *Blend all ingredients, place in a greased casserole, and bake at 400°F for 45 minutes.*

CORN-STUFFED TOMATOES

An interesting combination of two colorful vegetables.

2 Tbsps. chopped scallions
2 Tbsps. butter or margarine
8 tomatoes
½ tsp. salt
½ tsp. pepper
½ tsp. sugar
½ tsp. dried thyme
10 oz. frozen corn, thawed
4 Tbsps. bread crumbs

Yields 8.

- *Sauté scallions in butter or margarine.*
- *Cut off tops of tomatoes, scoop out pulp, and set pulp aside.*
- *Sprinkle inside of tomatoes with a dash of salt and place upside down on paper towels to drain.*
- *Combine sautéed scallions, tomato pulp, salt, pepper, sugar, thyme, and thawed corn.*
- *Place pulp mixture in a saucepan, and cook for about 5 minutes.*
- *Blend in bread crumbs, and stuff tomato shells with mixture.*
- *Place stuffed tomatoes on a greased baking dish, and bake at 400°F for 15 minutes.*

TOMATO AND EGG

If you're preparing a brunch I recommend this.

1 large onion, chopped
½ green pepper, diced
2 Tbsps. oil
20 oz. canned whole tomatoes, chopped small
1 tsp. salt
⅛ tsp. pepper
4 eggs

Yields 6 servings.

- *In a saucepan, sauté onion and green pepper in oil.*
- *Add tomatoes, salt, and pepper, and simmer for about 20 minutes.*
- *Just before serving, add whole raw eggs to vegetable mixture, and stir gently, breaking the egg yolks.*
- *Cover mixture and simmer for about 10 minutes.*

KREFSIAH
(Swiss Chard)

A delicious way to eat the Swiss chard at the Rosh Hashanah meal.

1 onion, chopped
2 Tbsps. oil
1 cup celery, chopped
1 bunch Swiss chard, cleaned well and chopped
10 oz. canned chickpeas
1 tsp. salt
⅛ tsp. pepper

Yields 4 servings.

- *Lightly sauté onion in oil.*
- *Add celery and simmer for 5 minutes.*
- *Add Swiss chard, chickpeas, salt, and pepper to onion-celery mixture.*
- *Cook, covered, on low flame for 30 minutes.*
- *Serve hot or cold.*

MEAT DISHES

Beef Stroganoff   85
Chili Con Carne   89
Eggplant Mechshe (Stuffed Eggplant)   90
Fried Edgeh (Meat Omelet)   91
Green Pepper, Onion, and Tomato Mechshe   92
Pepper Steak   97
Pickled Corned Beef and Cabbage   88
Rolled Kibbe with Cherries   94
Shish Kebab   99
Stuffed Breast of Veal with Mushrooms   101
Stuffed Cabbage   87
Stuffed Eggplant Rolls   86
Stuffed Grape Leaves   93
Stuffed Zucchini   102
Sul Ajon (Ground Meat on a Skewer)   99
Sweet-and-Sour Meatballs   96
Sweet-and-Sour Tongue   98
Sweetbreads and Mushrooms   95
Veal Française   100

MEAT DISHES

BEEF STROGANOFF

When a kosher restaurant in Queens was going out of business, my sister asked the owner for this recipe. His loss is our gain.

1½ lbs. sliced minute steak
4 Tbsps. margarine
1 onion, sliced
1 clove garlic, crushed
1 10 oz. can tomato soup
½ cup water
1 packet vegetable broth powder
1 tsp. salt
2 Tbsps. cornstarch dissolved in 4 Tbsps. water
½ lb. mushrooms, sliced
¼ cup non-dairy creamer

Yields 4 servings.

- *Brown meat in margarine.*
- *Remove meat, and brown onion and garlic.*
- *Return meat to onion mixture, and add tomato soup, water, vegetable broth powder, and salt.*
- *Bring mixture to a boil, and simmer for 30 minutes.*
- *Add mushrooms and cornstarch solution, and cook for an additional 10 minutes.*
- *Just before serving, add non-dairy creamer and reheat.*
- *Serve over rice or noodles.*

STUFFED EGGPLANT ROLLS

My son's mother-in-law, Lottie Chalom, is a chef par excellence who is hired to cook for parties. This is one of her favorites.

3 medium eggplants
coarse salt
1 Tbsp. oil for frying
3 Tbsps. rice
½ lb. ground beef
1 tsp. allspice
½ tsp. cinnamon
1 tsp. salt
6 Tbsps. water
½ cup water

Yields 10 servings.

- *Peel eggplants and slice lengthwise into slices ¼ inch thick.*
- *Spread eggplant slices on a flat surface, sprinkle with coarse salt, and let stand for 30 minutes.*
- *Pat dry with paper towels.*
- *Fry eggplant slices in hot oil, or broil (brush each slice with oil) until lightly browned, and let drain on paper towels.*
- *Soak rice in a bowl of hot water for 15 minutes. Drain.*
- *Combine rice, meat, allspice, cinnamon, salt, and the 6 tablespoons of water.*
- *Place 1 tablespoon of the meat mixture onto each eggplant slice, and roll up.*
- *Place eggplant rolls in casserole, seam side down, and add the half-cup of water.*
- *Bake, covered, at 350°F for 45 minutes to 1 hour.*

STUFFED CABBAGE

A blend of East and West — the sauce came from an Ashkenazi friend, and the stuffing is Sephardic. You will have a captive audience.

1 large cabbage

<u>Filling</u>

6 Tbsps. rice
1 lb. ground beef
2 tsps. allspice
2 tsps. salt
1 Tbsp. oil
1 tsp. cinnamon
½ cup water
2 Tbsps. chopped parsley

<u>Sauce</u>

2 Tbsps. oil
2 onions, sliced
2 cloves garlic
8 oz. tomato sauce
14 oz. canned tomatoes
⅓ cup brown sugar
⅓ cup raisins
1 tsp. salt
juice of 2 lemons
dash of white pepper

Yields 8–10 servings.

- **To prepare cabbage:** Place cabbage in the freezer for at least 2 days.
- Remove cabbage from freezer and allow to thaw for several hours. (Alternatively, thaw it by rinsing in the sink.)
- Remove center core and separate leaves.
- **To prepare filling:** Soak rice in a bowl of hot water for 15 minutes. Drain.
- Combine rice with ground meat, allspice, salt, oil, cinnamon, water, and parsley.
- Place 1 tablespoon of meat filling in center of each cabbage leaf and roll tightly, folding in each end.
- Place cabbage rolls, seam side down, in a saucepan.
- **To prepare sauce:** Brown onion and garlic in oil.
- Add tomato sauce, tomatoes, brown sugar, raisins, salt, lemon juice, and white pepper to onion and garlic mixture.
- Pour sauce over cabbage rolls.
- Place a small plate on top of cabbage rolls, cover saucepan, bring to a boil, and simmer for 1 hour.

PICKLED CORNED BEEF AND CABBAGE

An Irish dish loved by all cultures.

3 to 4 lbs. pickled corned beef

1 cabbage, cut into wedges

1 lb. carrots, peeled and cut in half

Yields 4–6 servings.

- *Cover corned beef with water, cover saucepan, and bring to a boil.*
- *Discard water, cover corned beef again with cold water, bring to a boil, and simmer for 2 hours.*
- *When corned beef is tender, remove from water.*
- *Add cabbage and carrots to water, and simmer for 15 minutes. Drain.*
- *Slice corned beef, and serve with cabbage and carrots.*

CHILI CON CARNE

Chili with a difference. What makes it special is the garnish on the chili. Popular through the ages and quite easy to prepare.

1 large onion, diced
2 cloves garlic, minced
2 Tbsps. oil
½ lb. ground beef
14 oz. canned tomatoes
8 oz. tomato sauce
1 Tbsp. chili powder
½ Tbsp. coarse salt
16 oz. canned kidney beans, washed and drained
2 scallions, chopped
1 hard-boiled egg, chopped
Chinese noodles

Yields 4–6 servings.

- *Sauté onion and garlic in oil until transparent.*
- *Add ground meat. Stir and cook until browned.*
- *Add tomatoes, tomato sauce, chili powder, salt, and kidney beans to meat mixture.*
- *Bring to a boil, and simmer for about 45 minutes.*
- *Top with chopped scallion, chopped egg, and Chinese noodles.*
- *Serve over rice or noodles.*

EGGPLANT MECHSHE
(Stuffed Eggplant)

The dried eggplant may be purchased at Middle Eastern groceries. The combination of the dry and fresh eggplant is quite unusual.

12 dried eggplants

1 large eggplant, sliced into ½-inch rounds

1 tsp. coarse salt

<u>Meat Filling</u>

½ lb. ground meat

3 Tbsps. rice

8 oz. canned chickpeas

1½ tsps. allspice

½ tsp. cinnamon

1 tsp. salt

6 Tbsps. water

2 Tbsps. parsley

1 cup water

1 tsp. allspice

1 tsp. salt

Yields 6 servings.

- *Boil dried eggplants for 10 minutes. Drain.*
- *Brush fresh eggplant slices with oil, and sprinkle with coarse salt.*
- *Broil eggplant slices on both sides until lightly browned.*
- *Soak rice in hot water for 15 minutes, and then drain.*
- *Thoroughly combine meat, drained rice, chickpeas, 1½ teaspoons allspice, cinnamon, 1 teaspoon salt, parsley, and 6 tablespoons water.*
- *Stuff each dried eggplant with meat mixture, about three-quarters full.*
- *Line the bottom of a saucepan with half of the broiled eggplant slices. Place stuffed eggplants close together over the eggplant slices, and top with remaining slices.*
- *Add 1 cup water mixed with 1 teaspoon allspice and 1 teaspoon salt.*
- *Cover eggplant with a small plate and cover pot.*
- *Boil for 5 minutes on a high flame, lower flame, and simmer for 1½ hours.*

FRIED EDGEH
(Meat Omelet)

On Friday afternoons, my mother would prepare these meat patties in pita bread with sliced tomatoes. Great on picnics.

½ lb. ground beef
4 eggs
2 Tbsps. matzah meal
¼ onion, chopped
3 Tbsps. chopped parsley
1 tsp. allspice
½ tsp. cinnamon
1 tsp. salt
½ cup oil for frying

Yields 4–6 servings.

- *Thoroughly combine all ingredients except for oil.*
- *Heat oil in skillet.*
- *Place 1 tablespoon of mixture at a time into skillet and turn until both sides are golden brown.*
- *Drain on paper towels.*

GREEN PEPPER, ONION, AND TOMATO MECHSHE

These three stuffed vegetables may be cooked together in a casserole. The colors give this dish great eye appeal.

4 large green peppers

Filling

6 Tbsps. rice
1 lb. ground beef
2 tsps. allspice
1 tsp. cinnamon
2 tsps. salt
½ cup water
1 Tbsp. oil
3 Tbsps. parsley

Sauce

½ cup water
½ cup tamarind sauce
juice of 2 fresh lemons
1 tsp. sugar
1 tsp. salt

Yields 6–8 servings.

- *Halve green peppers lengthwise. Remove seeds.*
- *Soak rice in hot water for 15 minutes. Drain.*
- *Combine filling ingredients, and fill green pepper halves with mixture.*
- *Place stuffed peppers, filling side down, in a 3-quart casserole.*
- *Mix together sauce ingredients, and pour over stuffed peppers.*
- *Cover casserole, and bake at 350°F for 1 hour.*
- **Variation:** *The same filling and sauce may be used for stuffed onions or tomatoes.*
- *For onions: Boil large Spanish onions until soft. Slice halfway through each onion, and separate each onion layer. Put stuffing in each layer, and roll up.*
- *For tomatoes: Cut tops off plum tomatoes, scoop out pulp, and fill.*

STUFFED GRAPE LEAVES

A classic Middle Eastern dish with a unique, delicious flavor.

1 16 oz. jar grape leaves*

<u>Filling</u>
6 Tbsps. rice
1 lb. ground beef
2 tsps. allspice
1 tsp. cinnamon
2 tsps. salt
1 Tbsp. oil
½ cup water
3 Tbsps. chopped parsley

<u>Sauce</u>
½ cup tamarind sauce
juice of 1 lemon
1 tsp. salt
2 cloves garlic, chopped
1 tsp. sugar
1 tsp. dried mint (see Food Prep. Tips, p. 16)
1 cup water
½ lb. apricots dried or canned

- Drain liquid from grape leaves, and wash well in cold water.
- Soak rice in hot water for 15 minutes. Drain.
- Combine filling ingredients, mixing well.
- Spread out each grape leaf, and remove the stem. Place 1 tablespoon of meat mixture at the bottom edge and roll up, folding in the sides.
- Place stuffed grape leaves close together in a saucepan.
- Combine sauce ingredients, and pour some of the sauce over the grape leaves. Top with some apricots.
- Repeat in layers.
- Place a small plate on the grape leaves and cover the pot.
- Bring to a boil, and simmer for 1½ hours.

* Be sure to purchase grape leaves with reliable kashrut supervision.

ROLLED KIBBE WITH CHERRIES

A very exotic dish with a sweet and sour sauce.

Filling
1 lb. kibbe meat (chopped beef and ground rice)
¾ lb. ground beef
1 clove garlic
1 tsp. salt
1 tsp. allspice
1 tsp. cinnamon
⅓ cup chopped walnuts

Sauce
1 16 oz. can dark sweet pitted cherries
¼ cup tamarind sauce
juice of 2 lemons
1 Tbsp. tomato paste
1 tsp. sugar
1 tsp. salt

Yields 10–12 servings.

- *Buy kibbe meat from Sephardic kosher butcher.*
- *Combine ground beef, garlic, salt, allspice, cinnamon, and walnuts.*
- *Divide kibbe meat into 2 equal parts.*
- *Using a rolling pin, roll out kibbe meat into a thin rectangle, about 11 by 8 inches in size.*
- *Spread half of meat filling evenly over surface of each kibbe rectangle.*
- *Roll up each rectangle, jellyroll fashion.*
- *Drain cherries, reserving the liquid.*
- *Mix together tamarind sauce, cherry liquid, tomato paste, sugar, lemon juice, and salt.*
- *Place rolled kibbe in a casserole, and pour sauce on top.*
- *Cover casserole and bake at 375°F for 1 hour.*
- *Slice kibbe rolls diagonally, and add drained cherries to casserole.*
- *Bake for an additional 15 minutes, uncovered.*

SWEETBREADS AND MUSHROOMS

A delicacy served at catered affairs. Now it can be made at home.

1½ lbs. sweetbreads
1 tsp. salt
½ tsp. pepper
½ tsp. paprika
½ cup flour
2 Tbsps. oil
1 onion, sliced
1 lb. fresh mushrooms
1 cup water

Yields 6–8 servings.

- *Pour 8 cups of boiling water over sweetbreads, soak for 4 to 8 minutes, and drain.*
- *Peel away thin membrane covering sweetbreads, and cut sweetbreads into 1- to 1½-inch cubes.*
- *Season sweetbreads with salt, pepper, and paprika, and coat with flour.*
- *Sauté onions in oil until almost brown.*
- *Add sweetbreads to onions, and continue sautéing until golden.*
- *Add whole mushrooms, and 1 cup of water.*
- *Cover and simmer for 1 hour.*

SWEET-AND-SOUR MEATBALLS

A hit with everyone who is a meatball lover. Fabulous for parties or for dinner. May be served on a bed of rice.

Meatballs
1 lb. ground beef
¾ cup bread crumbs
1 egg
1½ tsps. garlic powder
1½ tsps. salt
½ tsp. pepper
1 tsp. allspice

Sauce
2 cups orange juice
1 cup apricot juice, or ½ cup chopped dried apricots
16 oz. canned chunk pineapple, packed in its own juice
3 Tbsps. honey
1 Tbsp. brown sugar
1 lemon, sliced
¼ cup raisins
3 Tbsps. ketchup

Yields 18–20 meatballs.

- *Combine meat, bread crumbs, egg, garlic powder, salt, pepper, and allspice.*
- *Shape mixture into walnut-size balls, and set aside.*
- *Combine sauce ingredients in a saucepan, and bring mixture to a boil.*
- *Add meatballs to sauce, cover, and simmer for 1 hour.*

PEPPER STEAK

A variation of the Chinese steak dish. A pleasant change from the average stew.

- 1 large onion, sliced
- 2 cloves garlic, sliced
- 2 Tbsps. oil
- 1 lb. minute steak, sliced
- 1 large green pepper, diced
- 2 stalks celery, diced
- 1 cup Chinese marinade (duck sauce)
- 1 Tbsp. ketchup
- 10 oz. fresh mushrooms, sliced
- 12 oz. canned bamboo shoots
- 1 small can water chestnuts

Yields 3–4 servings.

- *Sauté onion and garlic in oil until transparent.*
- *Add steak and brown.*
- *Add green pepper and celery to steak mixture, and immediately add marinade and ketchup. Simmer for 1 hour.*
- *Add mushrooms, bamboo shoots, and water chestnuts, simmer an additional 10 minutes, and serve.*

SWEET-AND-SOUR TONGUE

We use this for Rosh Hashanah. The sauce makes it particularly tasty.

2 to 3 lbs. tongue (not pickled)
2 tsps. salt
1 whole medium onion

Sauce
2 onions, thinly sliced
2 cloves garlic, minced
2 Tbsps. oil
14 oz. canned whole tomatoes
8 oz. tomato sauce
⅓ cup brown sugar
juice of 2 lemons
⅓ cup raisins
1 tsp. coarse salt
¼ tsp. white pepper

Yields 8–10 servings.

- *Put tongue in a saucepan, cover with water, add 2 teaspoons of salt and a whole onion, and bring to a boil.*
- *Cook 1½ to 2 hours, until soft.*
- *While tongue is cooking, sauté onion and garlic in oil.*
- *Add remaining sauce ingredients, and mix.*
- *Remove tongue from saucepan, and rinse in cold water.*
- *Carefully peel off outer skin, and cut away bones and gristle.*
- *Slice tongue on diagonal, and arrange in a casserole.*
- *Pour sauce over sliced tongue, and bake at 350°F for 35 minutes.*

SUL AJON
(Ground Meat on a Skewer)

May be barbecued as well as broiled and eaten with pita bread. Add Syrian style salad also.

1 lb. ground beef
2 Tbsps. matzah meal
1 tsp. allspice
1 tsp. cinnamon
¼ cup fresh parsley
1 tsp. salt

Yields 4–6 servings.

- *Mix together all ingredients.*
- *Divide into 6 to 8 equal portions.*
- *Form each portion into an oblong shape.*
- *Place a skewer through each portion, and broil for about 6 minutes, rotating skewers to ensure even cooking.*

SHISH KEBAB

What a treat for those who love barbecues and for those who are fortunate enough to be invited.

2 lbs. minute steak
2 medium onions, quartered (or 6 small whole ones)
1 tsp. garlic powder
1 tsp. salt
1 tsp. paprika
12 cherry tomatoes
6 skewers

Yields 6 skewers.

- *Remove center vein from steak, and cut steak into bite-size chunks.*
- *On each skewer place 1 tomato, 3 meat chunks, 1 onion quarter, 3 more meat chunks, and 1 more tomato.*
- *Season with garlic powder, salt, and paprika.*
- *Broil meat skewers on a grill, rotating the skewers, for about 5 minutes.*

VEAL FRANÇAISE

I must admit that this is one of my best veal recipes. Enjoy!

1 lb. shoulder veal, thinly sliced
salt
pepper
1 tsp. paprika
flour
2 eggs, beaten with 1 Tbsp. water
2 Tbsps. oil
1 cup chicken broth
1 Tbsp. margarine
1 Tbsp. fresh lemon juice
1 lemon, sliced
parsley for garnish

Yields 4 servings.

- *Sprinkle salt, pepper, and paprika on veal.*
- *Dredge veal slices lightly in flour, and dip each slice in egg mixture.*
- *Sauté veal quickly in hot oil until golden brown, about 1 minute on each side.*
- *Discard oil, add broth and margarine to veal, and cook on high heat for 3 to 4 minutes.*
- *Add lemon juice and lemon slices, and garnish with parsley.*

STUFFED BREAST OF VEAL WITH MUSHROOMS

Slow cooking for a few hours makes this dish crispy and brown. It's one of our staple foods.

3 to 4 lbs. breast of veal, with pocket

<u>Stuffing</u>
3 Tbsps. rice
½ lb. ground beef or veal
1 tsp. allspice
½ tsp. cinnamon
½ tsp. coarse salt
¼ cup water

2 Tbsps. oil
1 tsp. allspice
1 tsp. salt
1½ cups water
2 lbs. fresh mushrooms

Yields 6–8 servings.

- *Soak rice in hot water for 15 minutes. Drain.*
- *Combine ground meat, rice, allspice, cinnamon, coarse salt, and ¼ cup of water.*
- *Loosely stuff meat mixture into pocket of each veal breast.*
- *In 3 places, slit top of each veal breast through to stuffing.*
- *Sprinkle oil on veal, and season with allspice and salt.*
- *Place veal in a roasting pan. Add 1 cup of water.*
- *Bake uncovered at 450°F for 30 minutes, basting every 10 minutes, until brown.*
- *Add ½ cup of water to pan and place mushrooms around veal.*
- *Lower oven temperature to 250°F, cover pan, and bake for an additional 2 to 2½ hours, basting every 20 minutes. Add more water if necessary.*

STUFFED ZUCCHINI

This is very appealing, especially with the added dried apricots.

10 small zucchini, 4 to 5 inches long

Stuffing

6 Tbsps. rice

1 lb. ground shoulder steak

2 tsps. allspice

1 tsp. cinnamon

2 tsps. coarse salt

⅔ cup water

1 Tbsp. oil

2 Tbsps. chopped parsley

Sauce #1

juice of 2 lemons

2 cloves garlic, minced

1 tsp. coarse salt

1 tsp. dried mint (see page 16)

1 tsp. sugar

1 cup water

Sauce #2

4 Tbsps. tamarind sauce

juice of 1 lemon

1 tsp. salt

1 tsp. sugar

10 oz. dried apricots

Yields 6–10 servings.

- *Wash zucchini and scrub with a vegetable brush.*
- *Cut off both ends of zucchini, and scoop out as much pulp as possible. (The zucchini can be halved before scooping out the pulp.) The pulp may be refrigerated or frozen and used for other recipes.*
- *Soak rice in hot water for 15 minutes. Drain. Combine stuffing ingredients, and blend well.*
- *Loosely stuff each zucchini ¾ full.*
- *Place zucchini close together in a pot, layering them.*
- *Any leftover stuffing mixture may be made into meatballs and placed on top of the zucchini.*
- *Combine sauce ingredients, pour over zucchini, and place a small plate or pot lid on top of zucchini.*
- *Cover and bring to a boil.*
- *Reduce flame to low, and simmer for 1½ hours.*
- *Alternatively, zucchini may be baked at 350°F for 1½ hours.*

CHICKEN DISHES

Apricot-Prune Chicken   112
Chicken à la King   110
Chicken and Potatoes   106
Chicken and Spaghetti   108
Chicken and Stuffed Eggplant   107
Chicken Pot Pie   105
Chicken Sesame   109
Oven-Fried Chicken   109
Poultry Stuffing   111

CHICKEN POT PIE

This dish charms the younger generations.

1 whole 3 to 4 lb. chicken
4 cups water
2 tsps. salt
¼ tsp. pepper
3 carrots, sliced
3 potatoes, cubed
3 onions, cubed
1 cup frozen peas
½ cup flour
½ cup water

<u>Pie Crust</u>
1½ cups flour
½ cup solid shortening or margarine
¼ cup ice water

Yields 6–8 servings.

- *Clean chicken thoroughly by rubbing with lemon and salt. Rinse.*
- *Place chicken in a pot with the 4 cups of water, salt, and pepper.*
- *Bring to a boil, lower flame, and simmer for 30 minutes.*
- *Add carrots, potatoes, and onions to pot, and simmer for an additional 30 minutes. Add peas.*
- *Remove chicken from pot and let cool.*
- *Bone the chicken, and cut into 1½- to 2-inch chunks.*
- *Dissolve flour in the half cup of water.*
- *Stir flour mixture into soup on a low flame until liquid thickens.*
- *Turn off stove, add cut up chicken, and mix.*
- **To prepare pie crust:** *In a food processor, mix flour and shortening or margarine.*
- *Add ice water gradually until mixture forms a ball of dough.*
- *Roll out between 2 pieces of waxed paper to fit over a large pyrex bowl.*
- *Place chicken mixture into the pyrex bowl, and cover with the pie crust.*
- *Bake at 375°F for 30 minutes, or until crust is golden brown.*

CHICKEN AND POTATOES

Without chicken and potatoes it would not be a Friday night meal.

1 whole 4 lb. chicken
1 Tbsp. oil
1 tsp. coarse salt
½ tsp. paprika
¼ tsp. pepper
1 cup water
3 lbs. potatoes, cut into cubes
oil for frying
1 tsp. allspice
1 tsp. salt

Yields 6–8 servings.

- *Clean chicken well by rubbing with lemon and coarse salt inside and outside. Rinse well.*
- *Make a paste with the oil, coarse salt, paprika, and pepper.*
- *Rub the inside and outside of chicken with the paste.*
- *Place chicken, uncovered, in a roasting pan with 1 cup of water.*
- *Bake at 500°F for 20 to 30 minutes, until browned. Baste often.*
- *Deep fry potatoes in oil until lightly browned.*
- *Remove potatoes from saucepan, and place on a paper towel to drain.*
- *Sprinkle salt and allspice over potatoes.*
- *Surround chicken with the potatoes in the roasting pan.*
- *Add ½ cup of water to the roasting pan and bake covered at 350°F for an additional 1½ hours.*

CHICKEN AND STUFFED EGGPLANT

This combination is very popular in my community and is often served at dinner parties.

1 whole 4 lb. chicken
1 Tbsp. oil
1 tsp. salt
1 Tbsp. garlic powder
1 Tbsp. paprika
1 large eggplant
12 small eggplants for filling

Filling
6 Tbsps. rice
1 lb. ground beef
2 tsps. allspice
1 tsp. cinnamon
1 tsp. coarse salt
1 Tbsp. oil
½ cup water

Yields 8–10 servings.

- *Clean chicken well by rubbing with lemon and coarse salt inside and out. Rinse well.*
- *Make a paste with the oil, salt, garlic powder, and paprika, and rub entire chicken with the paste. Set aside.*
- *Peel and slice the large eggplant into ½-inch slices.*
- *Place eggplant slices on wax paper, lightly sprinkle with salt, and let sit for 30 minutes.*
- *Dry with paper towel.*
- *Brush each eggplant slice on both sides with oil, and broil until browned.*
- *Cut off stems of small eggplants and scoop out as much pulp as possible.*
- *Soak rice in hot water for 15 minutes. Drain.*
- *To prepare filling, combine meat, rice, allspice, cinnamon, salt, oil, and water.*
- *Stuff each eggplant about ¾ full with filling.*
- *Place chicken in a medium roasting pan, arranging stuffed eggplants around chicken and sliced eggplants on top.*
- *Bake covered at 450°F for 30 minutes.*
- *Lower oven temperature to 350°F, add 2 cups of water, and bake for an additional 2 hours until chicken is tender.*

CHICKEN AND SPAGHETTI

The boned chicken and the sauce with cinnamon is terrific.

1 whole 3 to 4 lb. chicken
2 cloves garlic, minced
2 Tbsps. oil
1 tsp. paprika
1 tsp. coarse salt
2 onions, sliced
½ cup water
1 lb. spaghetti

<u>Sauce</u>
8 oz. tomato sauce
10 oz. clear chicken broth
2 tsps. cinnamon
drippings from roast chicken, drained

Yields 6–8 servings.

- *Clean chicken by rubbing with lemon and salt inside and out. Rinse well.*
- *Make a paste of garlic, oil, paprika, and salt, and rub over entire chicken.*
- *Line the bottom of a roasting pan with the sliced onions, and place chickcen, breast side up, on top.*
- *Add ½ cup of water, and bake uncovered at 500°F for 30 minutes.*
- *Baste occasionally.*
- *Turn chicken over, adding more water if necessary.*
- *Cover and bake at 350°F for 50 to 60 minutes or until tender.*
- *When chicken has cooled, remove skin and bones and cut into pieces.*
- *Cook spaghetti according to package instructions. Add chicken pieces to spaghetti, and mix.*
- *Combine sauce ingredients, and pour over spaghetti and chicken.*
- *Bake covered at 400°F for 30 minutes. Uncover and bake an additional 15 minutes.*

CHICKEN DISHES

OVEN-FRIED CHICKEN

This is a novel way to serve chicken, especially if you love potato chips.

1 broiler, cut into eighths
2 cups crushed, salted potato chips
¼ tsp. garlic powder
⅛ tsp. pepper
¼ cup chopped parsley
½ cup melted margarine

Yields 3–4 servings.

- Wash chicken, and clean thoroughly by rubbing with lemon and coarse salt. Rinse well.
- Combine potato chips, garlic powder, pepper, and parsley. Dip chicken in melted margarine and then dredge chicken pieces in mixture.
- Place chicken pieces, skin side up, in a greased casserole and sprinkle with remaining potato chip mixture.
- Bake uncovered at 375°F for 30 to 45 minutes.

CHICKEN SESAME

This recipe was created by a friend of mine who is a great cook. It made a big hit.

3 lbs. chicken cutlets
12 oz. cornflakes
2 tsps. salt
1 tsp. garlic salt
2 tsps. paprika
½ tsp. pepper
¼ cup sesame seeds
3 eggs, slightly beaten
1 Tbsp. water
2 cups flour

Yields 10–12 servings.

- Wash chicken cutlets.
- Crumble cornflakes to make crumbs, and combine with salt, garlic salt, paprika, pepper, and sesame seeds.
- Cut chicken into bite-size pieces.
- Add water to beaten eggs, and mix.
- Dip chicken pieces into flour, then egg, and then into cornflake mixture.
- Deep fry chicken in oil for 1 minute. Drain on a rack.

CHICKEN À LA KING

A delicious recipe served at many catered affairs.

1 whole 3 to 4 lb. chicken
4 cups water
1 bay leaf
2 tsps. salt
½ tsp. pepper
2 cups sliced fresh mushrooms
2 Tbsps. oil
10 oz. frozen peas
4 oz. pimentos
½ cup flour
½ cup water

Yields 6–8 servings.

- *Wash chicken, and clean thoroughly by rubbing with lemon and coarse salt. Rinse well.*
- *In a saucepan, put chicken, 4 cups water, bay leaf, 1 teaspoon of salt, and pepper.*
- *Bring to a boil, lower flame, and cook for 1 hour.*
- *Remove chicken from saucepan, and strain soup.*
- *Discard skin and bones from chicken, and cut chicken into chunks.*
- *In a saucepan, sauté sliced mushrooms in oil.*
- *Add 4 cups of chicken soup, chicken chunks, 1 teaspoon salt, peas, and pimentos, to mushrooms.*
- *Bring mixture to a boil, and reduce flame to simmer.*
- *Dissolve flour in water.*
- *Stir flour mixture into chicken soup and vegetable mixture, and cook on a small flame until soup thickens, stirring constantly.*
- *Serve with rice and Chinese noodles.*

POULTRY STUFFING

This is a fantastic stuffing, and the women I have taught always tell me how their families eat it up.

3 onions, chopped

3 stalks celery, chopped

12 oz. mushrooms, sliced

3 cloves garlic, chopped

8 oz. canned water chestnuts, drained and sliced

1 cup margarine

1 day-old challah, cubed

2 eggs

10 oz. chicken broth

2 tsps. salt

2 tsps. poultry seasoning

½ tsp. pepper

½ cup chopped parsley

Yields 6–8 servings.

- *In a saucepan, sauté onions, celery, mushrooms, garlic, and water chestnuts in margarine for 10 to 15 minutes, until tender.*
- *Add remaining ingredients to sautéed vegetables, and mix.*
- *Pour mixture into a casserole, and bake, uncovered, at 400°F for 1 hour.*

APRICOT-PRUNE CHICKEN

Well worth the time and effort.

1 box frozen chicken drummettes (small drumsticks), or 1 broiler chicken cut into sixteenths, or 1 cornish hen cut into eighths

2 Tbsps. oil

½ cup water

3 Tbsps. tamarind sauce

3 Tbsps. strawberry jam

3 Tbsps. apricot jam

juice of 1 lemon

1 Tbsp. salt

1 tsp. sugar

¼ lb. pitted prunes

¼ lb. dried apricots

Yields 6 servings.

- *Defrost, wash, and clean chicken pieces.*
- *Fill a 2-quart saucepan with water ¾ full, bring water to a boil, and add chicken pieces, cooking for 1 minute. Drain and dry.*
- *Sauté chicken pieces in oil until brown. Transfer chicken to a saucepan.*
- *Combine remaining ingredients, and pour over chicken.*
- *Cover and simmer for about 1 hour.*
- *Transfer chicken and sauce to a 3-quart casserole and bake, uncovered, at 375°F for 15 minutes, until browned.*

FISH

Baked Whitefish   117
Broiled Fillet of Sole   116
Broiled Salmon   117
Fish with Tahini   115
Salmon or Tuna Fish Cakes   118

FISH WITH TAHINI

Tahini makes fish so very tasty.

2 lbs. lemon sole
2 Tbsps. oil
2 stalks celery, cut into large-size pieces
2 onions, quartered
2 tsps. salt
¼ tsp. pepper
6 Tbsps. parsley

<u>Tahini Sauce</u>
1 cup tahini paste
juice of 2 lemons
2 cloves garlic, crushed
1 tsp. cumin
½ tsp. salt
¼ cup cold water

Yields 8 servings.

- *Brush fish with oil, and place on foil in baking pan.*
- *Place celery and onion on top of fish.*
- *Sprinkle salt and pepper on top.*
- *Cover with foil and bake at 400°F for 18 minutes.*
- *Remove fish from oven and let cool. Discard onion and celery.*
- *Flake fish into bowl and add parsley.*
- *Combine tahini, lemon juice, garlic, cumin, salt, and water, and blend well in a mixer.*
- *Add 4 tablespoons tahini mixture to flaked fish, and mix gently.*
- *Form into the shape of a fish, and spread remainder of tahini mixture to cover.*
- *Use black olives for the "eye."*

BROILED FILLET OF SOLE

Easy to prepare, this dish is perfect food for the soul.

1 lb. fillet of lemon sole

1 lemon, peeled and cut into 8 slices

2 Tbsps. mayonnaise

1 Tbsp. Dijon mustard

Yields 3–4 servings

- *Wash and dry fish*
- *In a broiling pan, place lemon slices under the fish.*
- *Combine mayonnaise and mustard, mix well, and spread on top of fish.*
- *Preheat broiler.*
- *Broil fish 4 to 6 inches from heat source for about 8 minutes, or until done.*

BROILED SALMON

Absolutely delicious — everybody's favorite.

½ whole salmon fillet (approx 4 lbs.)
2 Tbsps. mayonnaise
1 Tbsp. Dijon mustard
juice of ½ lemon

Yields 10–12 servings.

- *Wash and dry salmon*
- *Combine mayonnaise, mustard, and lemon juice.*
- *Spread mayonnaise mixture on top of salmon.*
- *Broil fish 4 to 6 inches from heat source for about 15 minutes, or until done.*

BAKED WHITEFISH

This is something extra-special.

2–3 lbs. whole fresh whitefish, scaled and cleaned
2 Tbsps. oil
1 tsp. cinnamon
1 tsp. salt
¾ cup walnuts, chopped

Yields 3–4 servings.

- *Wash and dry fish.*
- *Mix together 1 tablespoon oil, ½ teaspoon cinnamon, and ½ teaspoon salt.*
- *Rub outside of fish with oil mixture.*
- *Mix walnuts with 1 tablespoon oil, ½ teaspoon cinnamon, and ½ teaspoon salt.*
- *Fill fish cavity with walnut mixture.*
- *Bake uncovered at 400°F for 30 to 40 minutes.*

SALMON OR TUNA FISH CAKES

An economical way to satisfy the family at dinner time.

2 6½ oz. cans salmon or tuna
2 medium potatoes
2 onions, chopped
2 Tbsps. oil
¼ cup parsley
2 eggs
½ cup bread crumbs
½ tsp. garlic powder
½ tsp. black pepper
½ tsp. paprika
2 cups cornflakes, crumbled

Yields 24 fish cakes.

- Peel potatoes and boil until soft, then mash potatoes.
- Sauté onions in oil.
- Mix salmon or tuna with sautéed onions.
- Add mashed potatoes, parsley, eggs, bread crumbs, and salt.
- Shape into patties.
- Mix cornflakes with garlic powder, pepper, salt, and paprika.
- Dip each patty into cornflake mixture on both sides.
- Bake on greased cookie sheet at 350°F for 20 to 25 minutes.

DAIRY DISHES

Baked Shells in Tomato Sauce   133
Basic Crêpes   123
Blintz Soufflé   121
Bulgur with Cheese   121
Eggplant-Cheese Rollups   124
Eggplant Parmesan in Tomato Sauce   125
Jibbon (Spinach Soufflé) in Crêpes   131
Kelsonaise (Cheese Ravioli)   126
Keskassoon   127
Lasagna with Cheese   128
Manicotti Crêpes   129
Mechshe B'leban (Dairy Zucchini Stuffed with Rice)   137
Noodle Pudding   130
Noodles with Tahini   127
Spaghetti Primavera   132
Spinach Ravioli   134
White Syrian Cheese   122
Ziti and Eggplant   135
Zucchini Parmesan   136

DAIRY DISHES

BULGUR WITH CHEESE

A healthy, delectable dairy delight. A nice change from rice or noodles.

1 large onion, chopped
2 cloves garlic, minced
2 Tbsps. oil
1½ cups water
1 Tbsp. coarse salt
1 cup coarse bulgur (cracked wheat)
10 oz. canned chickpeas
½ cup cottage cheese

Yields 4–6 servings.

- *In a saucepan, sauté onion and garlic in oil until tender.*
- *Add water and salt to onion mixture, and bring to a boil.*
- *Wash and drain bulgur.*
- *Add bulgur and chickpeas to onion mixture, and bring to a boil again.*
- *Cover and simmer for 40 minutes, or bake at 350°F for 40 minutes.*
- *Serve topped with cottage cheese.*

BLINTZ SOUFFLÉ

A scrumptious soufflé. Not for those who are counting calories (but you won't regret the splurge!).

6 frozen blintzes (any filling)
3 eggs
½ cup sour cream
3 Tbsps. sugar
2 tsps. vanilla
cooking spray

Yields 6 servings.

- *Coat a small casserole with cooking spray.*
- *Place blintzes, evenly spaced, in casserole.*
- *Mix well the eggs, sour cream, sugar, and vanilla, and pour over blintzes.*
- *Bake at 350°F for 1 hour.*

WHITE SYRIAN CHEESE

Who makes their own cheese? Those who see how simple it can be.

8 cups whole milk, or 4 cups low fat milk and 4 cups whole milk

1 tsp. kosher liquid cheese rennet

handkerchief or closely woven cheesecloth

2 Tbsps. coarse salt

Yields 1 pound.

- *Heat milk until lukewarm.*
- *Add liquid rennet to milk, and stir.*
- *Let mixture stand for 10 minutes, until it congeals.*
- *Stir mixture gently until liquid separates.*
- *Place cloth on top of pot.*
- *Using a cup, press down on top of cloth to remove as much liquid as possible.*
- *Place cloth in a shallow bowl and pour cheese into cloth.*
- *Sprinkle 1 tablespoon of salt over cheese.*
- *Gather cloth at the top, and squeeze out remaining liquid until cheese is firm and round. Remove cheese from cloth.*
- *Sprinkle ½ tablespoon of salt into a shallow bowl.*
- *Place cheese in the bowl, and sprinkle an additional ½ tablespoon over cheese. Refrigerate for 1 hour.*
- *Put cheese into a plastic bag with liquid from bowl.*
- *Will keep for about 6 days in the refrigerator. Do not freeze.*

OPTIONAL:
- *Slice 12 small stuffed olives. Add olives just before gently stirring milk mixture after it congeals. If adding olives, decrease salt by ¼ tablespoon each time salt is called for.*

BASIC CRÊPES

Easy to prepare and to have on hand for company. Crêpes can be served with a variety of fillings. See, for example, Manicotti Crêpes, Jibbon, and Orange Crêpes.

1½ cups flour
1 tsp. sugar
½ tsp. salt
3 eggs
1½ cups water or milk
2 Tbsps. butter or margarine, melted and cooled
cooking spray

Yields 40 crêpes.

- *Sift together flour, sugar, and salt.*
- *In a blender, mix eggs and milk or water for about 1 minute.*
- *Add cooled butter or margarine to egg mixture and stir.*
- *Add dry ingredients to egg mixture, and blend well.*
- *Refrigerate batter for 1 hour.*
- *Spray a 4-inch skillet with cooking spray and heat.*
- *Pour 1 tablespoon of batter into the skillet, and quickly tilt pan, spreading batter evenly over its bottom surface.*
- *Cook on low heat for about 30 seconds on the first side and 15 seconds on the second side.*
- *Remove crêpe from pan, and repeat the above procedure for remainder of batter.*
- *Batter can be prepared the night before and refrigerated until ready to use.*
- *Crêpes can be frozen by storing in layers, placing 2 pieces of wax paper between each layer.*

EGGPLANT-CHEESE ROLLUPS

Exotic eggplant rolled with tender loving care — and cheese.

2 medium eggplants
salt
¼ cup oil
½ lb. Muenster cheese, grated
2 cups ricotta cheese
1 egg
1 tsp. salt
⅛ tsp. pepper
2 Tbsps. chopped parsley

Sauce
8 oz. tomato sauce
1 cup water
tsp. oregano
½ tsp. kosher salt
¼ tsp. pepper

Yields 14 rollups.

- *Slice eggplant lengthwise into thin slices.*
- *Sprinkle salt lightly on each slice.*
- *Place eggplant slices on paper towels to drain excess liquid, and let stand for 30 minutes.*
- *Brush each slice with oil on both sides.*
- *Broil slices for a few minutes on each side until golden brown.*
- *Mix cheeses, egg, salt, pepper, and parsley.*
- *Place 1 heaping tablespoon of cheese mixture on bottom of each slice and roll up.*
- *Place rollups side by side in a casserole, seam side down.*
- *Combine sauce ingredients, pour over eggplant, cover casserole, and bake at 350°F for 25 minutes.*
- *Uncover and bake for an additional 10 minutes.*

EGGPLANT PARMESAN IN TOMATO SAUCE

A delightful Italian dish.

1 large onion, chopped
2 cloves garlic, minced
1 green pepper, chopped
2 Tbsps. olive oil
26 oz. canned tomatoes
8 oz. tomato sauce
2 Tbsps. tomato paste
1 tsp. oregano
½ tsp. salt
¼ tsp. pepper
1 tsp. sugar
2 eggplants
½ lb. mozzarella cheese, thinly sliced

Yields 8–10 servings.

- Sauté onion, garlic, and green pepper in oil for 5 minutes.
- Add tomatoes, tomato sauce, tomato paste, oregano, salt, pepper, and sugar.
- Bring sauce to a boil, lower heat, and simmer for 2 hours.
- Peel eggplant, and cut into ½-inch slices.
- Place eggplant slices on wax paper, sprinkle salt on each slice, and let stand for 30 minutes.
- Dry eggplant on paper towel.
- Brush eggplant slices with oil, and broil on each side for about 5 minutes.
- Cover the bottom of a 3-quart casserole with sauce, and arrange eggplant slices on top.
- Add a layer of mozzarella cheese. Cover the cheese with another layer of sauce, then eggplant slices, and then add another layer of cheese. Repeat layering until all ingredients are used up.
- Bake at 350°F for 40 to 50 minutes.

KELSONAISE
(Cheese Ravioli)

A new kind of ravioli. A praiseworthy pasta.

egg roll dough (3-inch rounds or squares)
1½ lbs. Muenster cheese, grated
3 eggs, slightly beaten
1 tsp. salt
1 tsp. baking powder
6 cups water
½ cup butter or margarine

Yields 60 ravioli.

- *Mix cheese, eggs, salt, and baking powder together. Blend well.*
- *Thaw out egg roll dough. Moisten edges of each round or square with water.*
- *Put 2 teaspoons of cheese mixture in center of each round or square.*
- *Fold dough in half, pressing edges together well.*
- *Bring water to a boil, and drop 8 to 10 kelsonaise into water.*
- *Boil for about 5 minutes and drain. Repeat procedure for remaining kelsonaise.*
- *Place kelsonaise in rows in a buttered 3-quart casserole. Dot with butter. (Cooked medium noodles may be added and baked in a casserole together with the kelsonaise.)*
- *Bake covered at 350°F for 30 minutes. Uncover and bake for an additional 15 minutes.*

DAIRY DISHES

KESKASSOON

A real Middle Eastern pasta dish.

1 large onion
3 Tbsps. oil
16 oz. Acini de Pepe or couscous
3½ cups water
10 oz. canned chickpeas
1½ Tbsps. salt

Yields 6 servings.

- *Sauté onion in oil for 4 to 5 minutes.*
- *Add pasta and sauté for about 7 more minutes.*
- *Add water, chickpeas, and salt.*
- *Cover saucepan, and bring mixture to a boil.*
- *Lower heat, and simmer for about 20 minutes, until liquid is almost completely absorbed.*
- *Bake in the saucepan at 325°F for 30 minutes.*
- *Turn off heat, and leave saucepan in oven for an additional 10 minutes.*

NOODLES WITH TAHINI

For a change of pace, Middle Eastern flavor meets the American noodle.

1 lb. ¼-inch wide noodles

Tahini
½ cup tahini
¼ cup water
1 clove garlic, crushed
½ tsp. salt
juice of 1 lemon
chopped parsley

Yields 6–8 servings.

- *Boil noodles according to package directions. Drain.*
- *Thoroughly combine tahini ingredients. Add to noodles just before serving, and mix well.*
- *Sprinkle with parsley.*

LASAGNA WITH CHEESE

Another Italian favorite. Quite filling and satisfying.

1 lb. lasagna noodles
2 eggs
1½ lbs. ricotta cheese
½ lb. mozzarella cheese cubed
¼ cup grated Parmesan cheese

Sauce

2 onions, diced
3 cloves garlic, crushed
2 Tbsps. olive oil
28 oz. canned tomatoes, strained and seeded
6 oz. tomato paste
1 cup water
1 whole carrot, peeled
1 bay leaf
1 Tbsp. salt
¼ tsp. pepper
2 tsps. dried basil

Yields 8 servings.

- *Fill a large saucepan with water, bring water to a boil, add lasagna noodles, and cook for 8 minutes.*
- *Drain noodles, and rinse in cold water.*
- *Place lasagna noodles around the rim of a pot to dry.*
- *Mix together eggs and cheeses, and set aside.*
- *Sauté onions and garlic in oil.*
- *Add tomatoes, tomato paste, water, carrot, bay leaf, salt, pepper, and basil to onion mixture.*
- *Bring sauce ingredients to a boil. Lower heat, and simmer for 1 hour.*
- *Discard carrot and bay leaf.*
- *Cover the bottom of a greased, 3-quart casserole with sauce.*
- *Place 5 strips of lasagna over sauce. Cover lasagna noodles with a thin layer of the cheese mixture.*
- *Repeat layering 2 more times.*
- *Bake at 350°F for 30 to 40 minutes.*

MANICOTTI CRÊPES

Unusual and delicious manicotti made with crêpes instead of pasta.

<u>Crêpes</u>
1½ cups flour
1 tsp. sugar
½ tsp. salt
3 eggs
1½ cups water or milk
2 Tbsps. butter or margarine, melted and cooled
cooking spray

<u>Filling</u>
16 oz. ricotta cheese
1 egg, slightly beaten
8 oz. cheddar cheese, grated
1 tsp. coarse salt
¼ tsp. pepper

<u>Sauce</u>
1 onion, diced
2 Tbsps. oil
8 oz. tomato sauce
1 cup water
1 bay leaf
½ tsp. coarse salt

Yields 30 crêpes.

- Sift together flour, sugar, and salt.
- Mix in blender eggs and water or milk.
- Add butter or margarine and flour, sugar, and salt mixture to egg mixture. Mix well.
- Let mixture stand for 1 hour. (Crêpe batter can be made the night before and refrigerated until ready to use.)
- Spray cooking spray on a 4-inch skillet and heat.
- Pour 1 tablespoon crêpe mixture into skillet and quickly tilt pan, spreading batter evenly over the surface.
- Fry batter on a low flame for 30 seconds on the first side and 15 seconds on the second side. (Unfilled crêpes may be frozen in stacks, separating each crêpe with 2 pieces of wax paper.)
- Blend ricotta cheese, egg, cheddar cheese, salt, and pepper.
- Fill center of each crêpe with 2 tablespoons of cheese mixture, fold over both sides, and roll up.
- Place crêpes in a casserole, seam side down.
- Sauté onion in oil until transparent.
- Add tomato sauce, water, bay leaf, and salt to onions. Bring to a boil, and simmer for about 15 minutes.
- Remove bay leaf, and pour sauce over crêpes.
- Bake covered at 350°F for 20 minutes.

NOODLE PUDDING

A side dish that may also be served as a rich dessert.

8 oz. medium noodles
8 oz. cottage cheese
8 oz. sour cream
1 tsp. vanilla
½ cup raisins
¼ cup butter, melted
½ cup sugar
⅓ cup milk
4 eggs, well beaten
10 oz. canned crushed pineapple, drained

Topping
4 cups cornflakes
1 Tbsp. sugar
½ tsp. cinnamon

Yields 8 servings.

- *Cook noodles as directed on package. Drain.*
- *Add cottage cheese, sour cream, vanilla, raisins, butter, sugar, milk, eggs, and crushed pineapple to noodles. Mix well.*
- *Pour noodle mixture into a 3-quart casserole.*
- *Crush cornflakes to make crumbs. Mix cornflake crumbs, sugar, and cinnamon, and sprinkle over noodle mixture.*
- *Bake at 350°F for 1 hour.*
- *May be prepared a day in advance. Can be reheated or served cold.*

JIBBON (Spinach Soufflé) IN CRÊPES

Flowerlike individual soufflés to grace your table. When time is short, it can be baked as a casserole without the crêpe.

Crêpes
1½ cups flour
1 tsp. sugar
½ tsp. salt
3 eggs
1½ cups water or milk
2 Tbsps. butter or margarine, melted and cooled
cooking spray

Filling
1 large onion, chopped
2 Tbsps. oil
20 oz. frozen spinach, thawed and well drained
5 eggs, slightly beaten
½ lb. Muenster cheese, grated
2 tsps. salt
½ tsp. pepper

Yields 24 crêpes.

- *Sift together flour, sugar, and salt.*
- *Mix eggs and water or milk in blender.*
- *Add butter or margarine and flour mixture to eggs. Mix well.*
- *Let mixture stand for at least 1 hour. (Crêpe batter can be made the night before and refrigerated until ready to use.)*
- *Spray cooking spray on the surface of a 4-inch skillet and heat.*
- *Pour 1 tablespoon of crêpe mixture into skillet. Quickly tilt pan to spread batter evenly over the surface.*
- *Fry batter on a low flame for 30 seconds on the first side and 15 seconds on the second side. (Unfilled crêpes may be frozen in stacks, separating each crêpe with 2 pieces of wax paper.)*
- *Sauté onion in oil.*
- *Combine remaining ingredients. Add onions.*
- *Place crêpes into a greased muffin tin.*
- *Fill each crêpe with 2 to 3 tablespoons of spinach mixture.*
- *Bake at 350°F for 30 minutes.*

SPAGHETTI PRIMAVERA

A tantalizing combination of pasta and vegetables.

1 lb. thin spaghetti
2 Tbsps. butter or margarine
3 Tbsps. oil
3 cloves garlic, minced
½ bunch broccoli florets
2 zucchini, cubed
10 oz. frozen peas
1 cup cut green beans
6 plum tomatoes, chopped
1 tsp. salt
1 tsp. oregano
1 tsp. basil
½ tsp. white pepper
1 tsp. chopped parsley
¼ to ⅓ cup grated Parmesan cheese

Yields 4–6 servings.

- *Cook spaghetti according to package instructions, and drain. Add butter or margarine, and mix.*
- *Sauté garlic in hot oil.*
- *Add broccoli, zucchini, peas, and green beans to garlic, and stir-fry for 4 minutes.*
- *Add tomatoes, salt, oregano, basil, white pepper, and parsley.*
- *Simmer vegetables until tomatoes are soft, about 4 minutes.*
- *Pour mixture over spaghetti.*
- *Serve topped with grated Parmesan cheese.*

BAKED SHELLS IN TOMATO SAUCE

A homemade sauce makes this dish extra special.

1 lb. box jumbo shells
1 lb. ricotta cheese
½ lb. cheddar cheese, grated
1 egg, slightly beaten
1 tsp. salt
½ tsp. pepper

<u>Sauce</u>
1 large onion, chopped
4 cloves garlic, minced
2 Tbsps. oil
28 oz. canned whole tomatoes
6 fresh or dried basil leaves, chopped
½ cup chopped parsley
1 tsp. salt
½ tsp. oregano
¼ tsp. pepper

Yields 8 servings.

- *Cook shells according to package directions. Drain.*
- *Mix together cheeses, egg, salt, and pepper.*
- *Fill shells with cheese mixture, and place in a 3-quart casserole.*
- **To prepare sauce:** *Sauté onion and garlic in oil until transparent.*
- *Mash tomatoes and add to onion mixture.*
- *Add basil, parsley, salt, oregano, and pepper.*
- *Cover mixture and simmer for 20 minutes.*
- *Pour sauce over shells. Cover and bake at 350°F for 30 minutes.*

SPINACH RAVIOLI

For spinach lovers, have yourselves a treat.

4 bunches thinly sliced scallions
2 Tbsps. oil
3 oz. cream cheese
10 oz. frozen chopped spinach, well drained
8 oz. Parmesan cheese
2 cups ricotta cheese
2 eggs
2 tsps. salt
½ tsp. pepper
1 pkg. egg roll dough, 3-inch squares or rounds

Sauce

1 large onion
5 cloves garlic, minced
2 Tbsps. oil
28 oz. canned tomatoes
2 Tbsps. chopped basil
¼ cup chopped parsley
½ tsp. oregano
1 tsp. salt
¼ tsp. pepper

Yields 50 ravioli.

- *Sauté scallions in oil for 5 minutes.*
- *Add cream cheese to scallion mixture and cook on low heat for 5 minutes.*
- *Remove mixture from flame. Add spinach, Parmesan and ricotta cheese, eggs, salt, and pepper.*
- *Moisten edges of egg roll rounds or squares.*
- *Fill center of each with one tablespoon of mixture and fold into a half circle or triangle, pressing edges tightly together.*
- *Bring a saucepan of water to a boil, drop 10 ravioli into boiling water, and cook for 3 to 5 minutes.*
- *Continue boiling remaining ravioli in the same manner.*
- *Place ravioli in a 3-quart casserole.*
- *Sauté onion and garlic in oil.*
- *Mash tomatoes and mix with basil, parsley, oregano, salt, and pepper.*
- *Add sautéed onion to mixture, combine thoroughly, and pour over ravioli.*
- *Cook covered at 350 °F for 25 minutes.*
- *Uncover and cook for an additional 10 minutes.*

ZITI AND EGGPLANT

A snappy tomato sauce dish.

8 oz. ziti
1 eggplant
½ cup butter or margarine, melted
1 cup shredded mozzarella cheese
¼ cup grated Parmesan cheese

Sauce

½ cup chopped onion
1 garlic clove, crushed
2 Tbsps. butter or margarine
16 oz. canned crushed tomatoes
1 tsp. oregano
½ tsp. salt
⅛ tsp. pepper
Yields 4 servings.

- *Cook ziti according to package instructions. Drain.*
- *Slice eggplant lengthwise into ⅓-inch slices.*
- *Brush both sides of eggplant slices with melted butter or margarine.*
- *Broil eggplant on each side until golden brown.*
- *Sauté onion and garlic in butter or margarine until golden.*
- *Add tomatoes, oregano, salt, and pepper to the onion mixture, and simmer for 15 minutes, until sauce thickens.*
- *Layer ziti in a 2-quart casserole.*
- *Pour half of the sauce over ziti, sprinkle with mozzarella cheese, and cover with the eggplant slices.*
- *Add the remaining sauce, and sprinkle Parmesan cheese on top.*
- *Bake at 350°F for 30 minutes, or until bubbly.*

ZUCCHINI PARMESAN

A new approach to Parmesan, substituting zucchini for eggplant.

4 medium zucchini
oil
salt
1 onion, chopped
2 cloves garlic, minced
2 Tbsps. oil
10 oz. marinara sauce
1 tsp. basil
½ tsp. oregano
1 tsp. salt
dash pepper
½ lb. Muenster cheese, grated

Yields 8–10 servings.

- *Clean zucchini with a vegetable brush.*
- *Cut each zucchini in 4 slices lengthwise.*
- *Brush each slice on both sides with oil, sprinkle each slice with salt, and broil on both sides until golden brown.*
- *Sauté onion and garlic in oil.*
- *Add marinara sauce, basil, oregano, salt, and pepper to onion mixture, and simmer for about 10 minutes.*
- *Cover the bottom of a 3-quart casserole with a thin layer of sauce.*
- *Cover the sauce with a layer of zucchini slices.*
- *Pour sauce over zucchini, and cover with cheese.*
- *Continue to layer zucchini, sauce, and cheese.*
- *Pour the remaining sauce on top and sprinkle with the rest of the cheese.*
- *Cover and bake at 350°F for 35 minutes.*
- *Uncover and bake for an additional 10 minutes.*

MECHSHE B'LEBAN
(Dairy Zucchini Stuffed with Rice)

An interesting and delectable dairy dish with or without yogurt.

1 cup rice

8 small and thin zucchini

½ cup canned chickpeas

½ cup butter, melted

½ tsp. dried mint (see Food Prep. Tips, p. 16)

2 tsps. salt

dash white pepper

1½ cups water

2 cloves garlic, minced

Yields 4–6 servings.

- *Soak rice in hot water for 15 minutes, and drain.*
- *Clean zucchini with a vegetable brush.*
- *Trim ends of zucchini (or cut zucchini in half), and scoop out pulp. (Zucchini pulp may be used instead of spinach in Spinach Soufflé recipe, p. 131.)*
- *Add chickpeas, butter, mint, salt, and white pepper to rice.*
- *Fill each zucchini ¾ full with the rice mixture.*
- *Place zucchini horizontally and close together in a medium-size pot.*
- *Pour water over zucchini, and sprinkle with minced garlic.*
- *Cover and simmer for 1 hour.*

DESSERTS

Almasyia (Cornstarch Pudding)   145
Apple Crisp   142
Apple Pie   141
Apricot Candy   144
Ataiyef (Stuffed Pancakes)   143
Baklava   147
Bizzard (Roasted Pumpkin Seeds)   148
Blueberry Muffins   146
Bread Pudding   145
Caramel Custard Flan   154
Carrot Cake   156
Cheese Danish   152
Chocolate Chip Cookies   155
Chocolate Mousse   149
Chocolate Mousse Pie   150
Coconut Candy   158
Cream Cheese Cake   151
Crumb Cake   153
Dairy Rugelach   176
Date and Nut Bread   148
Date Cakes   157
Deep Dish Peach Pie   171
Fruit Tart   181
Graham Cracker Roll   158

Graybeh (Butter Ring Cookies)   151
Hamantashen   159
Heavenly Hash   166
Ka'ak-Ib-Loz (Almond-Pistachio Rings)   162
Kanafe (Shredded Dough)   160
Kanafe Ring   161
Krabeeg (Marshmallow Fluff Cookies)   164
Lemon Meringue Pie   165
Mamoule (Nut-Filled Cookies)   167
Mixed Berries Salad   175
Orange Crêpes   168
Orange Fantasia   169
Passover Nut Cake   170
Passover Pistachio Cookies   174
Pecan Pie   172
Pineapple Nut Cake   173
Rice Pudding   175
Sponge Cake   179
Strawberry Compote   179
Strawberry Shortcake   177
Suttlage Fingers (Cornstarch Pudding Pastries)   178
Sweet Ka'ak (Crackers)   163
Thumbprint Cookies   180
Tropical Fruit Salad   170

APPLE PIE

Who doesn't like apple pie? Serve with ice cream or Tofutti.

<u>Piecrust</u>
1½ cups flour
½ cup butter or solid shortening
½ cup ice water

<u>Filling</u>
6 large Granny Smith apples
juice of 1 lemon
½ cup sugar
2 Tbsps. flour
1 tsp. cinnamon
2 Tbsps. butter or margarine

Yields 8 servings.

- *Mix flour and butter or shortening in a food processor or mixer.*
- *Add ice water to mixture until it forms a ball of dough. Set aside.*
- *Peel, core, and slice apples. Dip slices into lemon juice.*
- *Add sugar, flour, and cinnamon to apples. Blend well.*
- *Divide dough in half. Roll out one half of dough, and place in a 9-inch pie plate.*
- *Spoon apple slices into pie shell, and dot with butter or margarine.*
- *Roll out second half of dough, and place over apples. Flute edges of dough, and make a few slits in the top.*
- *Bake at 400°F for 50 minutes.*
- *The unbaked pie may be frozen. When ready to bake, do not thaw. Place it directly from the freezer to the oven. This eliminates any liquid forming due to thawing.*

APPLE CRISP

So simple, nothing can go wrong.

6 large Granny Smith apples
juice of 1 lemon
1 tsp. cinnamon
¾ cup raisins
¾ cup walnuts, chopped
½ cup brown sugar
¾ cup flour
6 Tbsps. butter or margarine

Yields 8–10 servings.

- *Grease a 3-quart casserole.*
- *Core, peel, and slice apples.*
- *Mix apple slices with lemon juice, cinnamon, walnuts, and raisins, and spread in the casserole.*
- *Combine sugar and flour.*
- *Cut butter or margarine into flour mixture and mix well.*
- *Spread flour mixture over apples.*
- *Bake at 350°F for 40 minutes or until browned.*
- *Serve with ice cream or whipped cream.*

ATAIYEF
(Stuffed Pancakes)

Good when you want something exotic and rich. Should be fried and served the same day. May be frozen before frying.

1 cup pancake mix
1 cup water

<u>Walnut Filling</u>
½ lb. chopped walnuts
1¼ Tbsps. sugar
2 Tbsps. butter or margarine
½ tsp. cinnamon

<u>Ricotta Filling</u>
2 cups ricotta cheese
2 Tbsps. sugar
½ tsp. cinnamon
cooking spray
oil for frying

<u>Syrup</u>
1 cup sugar
½ cup water
1 tsp. lemon juice
1 tsp. orange water

Yields 40 pancakes.

- Gently stir together pancake mix and water with a fork. Set aside.
- **For walnut filling:** Mix together walnuts, sugar, butter or margarine, and cinnamon.
- **For Ricotta filling:** Combine Ricotta cheese, sugar, and cinnamon.
- Spray cooking spray on a grill.
- Pour 1 tablespoon of pancake batter on grill. Cook on one side only.
- When bubbles form on surface of pancake, remove from grill and immediately place 1 teaspoon of filling in center of uncooked side.
- Fold pancake in half to form half-moon shape, firmly pinching sides together.
- Deep fry pancakes slowly until brown.
- **To prepare syrup:** Combine first three syrup ingredients, bring to a boil, and continue boiling for 4 minutes.
- Add orange water after syrup is cooked.
- Pour hot syrup over cooled, filled pancakes.

APRICOT CANDY

Wow! What a treat! Apricots at their best. People love this homemade candy.

1 lb. dried apricots
1 cup sugar
1 tsp. lemon juice
¼ cup shelled pistachio nuts

Yields 40 pieces.

- *Steam dried apricots in a double boiler for 20 to 30 minutes, until soft.*
- *Mix thoroughly apricots, sugar, and lemon juice in a food processor until it forms a paste.*
- *Put mixture in a small pot and cook on a medium flame, stirring constantly, for about 5 minutes.*
- *Soak pistachio nuts in hot water for 10 minutes. Drain, peel, and add to apricot mixture, mixing well.*
- *Wet hands in cold water, and spread mixture in a rectangular or square casserole.*
- *Let cool and keep candy exposed to air, uncovered, for two days.*
- *Cut into diamond shapes.*
- *May be frozen.*

DESSERTS

ALMASYIA
(Cornstarch Pudding)

A form of jello made only with cornstarch. The orange water gives this dessert a distinctive flavor.

9 cups water
1¼ cups sugar
1½ cups cornstarch
2 tsps. orange water
¼ cup pignolia nuts or shelled pistachio nuts

Yields 10–12 servings.

- Mix water, sugar, and cornstarch in a saucepan.
- Bring mixture to a boil, lower flame, and cook for 1½ to 2 hours, stirring frequently, until pudding is thickened.
- Remove pudding from flame, add orange water, and stir.
- If using pistachio nuts: Soak pistachio nuts in hot water for 10 minutes. Drain and peel.
- Pour pudding into a shallow bowl and sprinkle nuts on top.

BREAD PUDDING

A great way to use leftover challah.

½ challah, cut into chunks
½ cup raisins
2 cups milk
6 eggs
3 Tbsps. butter
1 tsp. vanilla extract
½ cup sugar
2 tsps. cinnamon

Yields 8 servings.

- Soak challah and raisins in milk for 15 minutes.
- Combine eggs, butter, vanilla, sugar, and cinnamon.
- Put bread mixture into a deep round casserole, and pour egg mixture on top.
- Bake at 350°F for 45 minutes.

BLUEBERRY MUFFINS

It seems like these scrumptious muffins have more blueberries than muffins.

3½ cups flour
2 Tbsps. baking powder
pinch of salt
1 cup sugar
5 eggs, slightly beaten
½ cup milk
5 oz. sweet butter or margarine, melted and cooled
4 to 5 cups fresh blueberries
cooking spray
sugar for topping

Yields 24 muffins.

- *Preheat oven to 425°F.*
- *Mix flour, baking powder, salt, and sugar in a bowl.*
- *Add eggs, milk, and butter or margarine to flour mixture.*
- *Mix batter by hand, being careful not to overmix.*
- *Wash and drain blueberries, and fold into batter.*
- *Grease muffin tins with cooking spray.*
- *Fill muffin cups to top with batter.*
- *Sprinkle sugar over unbaked muffins.*
- *Reduce heat to 400°F, and bake on middle rack of oven for 25 minutes, until golden brown.*
- *Cool for about 30 minutes before removing muffins from tins.*

BAKLAVA

Baklava at its best. A Middle Eastern dessert that's loved by all.

Baklava Syrup
2 cups sugar
1 cup water
1 tsp. lemon juice

1 lb. walnuts, chopped
4 Tbsps. confectioners' sugar
4 Tbsps. butter or margarine
2 tsps. orange water
1 lb. phyllo dough
1½ cups butter or margarine, clarified (see Food Prep. Tips, p. 15)

Yields 35–40 pastries.

- *Bring syrup ingredients to a boil. Stir, reduce heat, and simmer for 4 minutes. Let syrup cool, and refrigerate.*
- *Thoroughly combine nuts, sugar, the 4 tablespoons of butter or margarine, and orange water. Set aside.*
- *Cut phyllo dough in half widthwise, so that it measures 8½ by 11 inches. Wrap half of the phyllo dough in aluminum foil and refrigerate. Cover remaining phyllo dough with a dish towel.*
- *Brush bottom and sides of 3-quart casserole with clarified butter or margarine. Place in it 1 cut phyllo sheet and brush evenly with clarified butter or margarine. Continue layering all the unrefrigerated phyllo dough sheets and brushing with butter or margarine. Sprinkle the chopped nut mixture on top, pressing down firmly.*
- *Remove phyllo from refrigerator, and repeat layering and brushing with the second half of phyllo, coating the top layer well.*
- *Refrigerate the pastry for 30 minutes.*
- *Use a sharp knife to cut pastry into diamond-shape pieces, cutting only halfway through pastry.*
- *Bake at 350°F for 1 hour or until pastry is lightly browned.*
- *Pour cold syrup over hot baklava.*
- *Before baklava cools completely, cut through to separate pieces.*

DATE AND NUT BREAD

An old American standby. Serve with cream cheese.

8 oz. pitted, quartered dates
1 cup boiling water
½ cup sugar
2 Tbsps. butter or margarine
1 egg
1⅓ cups flour
1 tsp. baking powder
1 cup chopped walnuts

Yields 8–10 slices.

- *Cover dates with boiling water and soak for 20 minutes. Drain.*
- *Cream sugar, butter or margarine, and egg in a mixing bowl.*
- *Add flour, baking powder, walnuts, and dates to sugar mixture.*
- *Pour batter into a greased loaf pan.*
- *Bake at 350°F for 1 hour.*

BIZZARD
(Roasted Pumpkin Seeds)

They taste much better than the store-bought variety. A delicious Shabbat treat.

1 lb. pumpkin seeds
cold water
5 Tbsps. coarse salt

- *Put pumpkin seeds in a bowl, and cover with cold water.*
- *Add 2 tablespoons of the salt and soak for 2 hours or overnight.*
- *Drain and rinse seeds, and place in a large jellyroll pan.*
- *Add the remaining 3 tablespoons of salt to the seeds, and mix well.*
- *Bake at 400°F for 1½ hours, stirring seeds every 15 minutes.*
- *Let seeds cool, and refrigerate in jars.*

CHOCOLATE MOUSSE

Serve with whipped cream. Heavenly!

6 oz. semi-sweet chocolate chips

6 eggs, separated

1 cup heavy cream or pareve dessert whip

½ tsp. vanilla extract

Yields 8 servings.

- *Put chocolate chips in top part of a double boiler, and cook on very low flame, stirring frequently until chips are melted.*
- *Let melted chips cool for 5 minutes.*
- *Beat egg yolks in a mixer. Add chocolate and blend well.*
- *Beat cream or dessert whip until stiff. Add vanilla.*
- *Beat egg whites until stiff.*
- *Fold both cream and egg whites into chocolate and egg mixture until well blended.*
- *Pour into a bowl and refrigerate.*
- *May be prepared up to 2 days in advance.*

CHOCOLATE MOUSSE PIE

A chocolate lover's delight. May be frozen before serving.

Crust

3 cups ground chocolate wafers

½ cup margarine, melted

Filling

16 oz. semi-sweet chocolate

2 eggs

4 egg yolks

2 cups whipping cream or pareve whipped topping

6 Tbsps. confectioners' sugar

4 egg whites

Yields 12–14 servings.

- *Mix together ground wafers and margarine and press into a 10-inch springform pan.*
- *Refrigerate crust for 30 minutes.*
- *Melt chocolate and let cool. Add whole eggs to chocolate, beating well. Add egg yolks.*
- *Whip together cream or pareve whipped topping. (If using pareve whipped topping, do not add confectioners' sugar.)*
- *Whip egg whites until stiff. Add 2 tablespoons of whipped cream and 2 tablespoons of whipped egg white to chocolate mixture, and mix.*
- *Fold the remaining whipped egg white and whipped cream into chocolate mixture.*
- *Pour the mousse over the crust, and refrigerate for 6 hours or overnight.*

DESSERTS

CREAM CHEESE CAKE

Real yummy. Made with natural ingredients. A great cake for company.

6 Tbsps. butter, melted
20 graham crackers, crushed
24 oz. sour cream
16 oz. cream cheese
3 eggs
1 cup sugar
1 tsp. vanilla extract
1 tsp. almond extract

Yields 10–12 servings.

- Thoroughly combine butter and graham cracker crumbs.
- Press crumb mixture into a 10-inch springform pan.
- Thoroughly mix remaining ingredients in a food processor or blender.
- Pour mixture over graham cracker crust, and bake at 375°F for 40 minutes.
- Turn off oven, and leave cake in oven for an additional 10 minutes.
- Remove cake from oven, and let cool.

GRAYBEH   (Butter Ring Cookies)

These rich cookies seem to melt to your mouth as you anticipate the next bite.

1 cup sugar
1 cup clarified butter, cooled (see Food Prep. Tips, p. 15)
3 cups flour
pistachio nuts or almonds, peeled

Yields 40 biscuits.

- Cream sugar and butter well in a mixer. Add flour and mix.
- Shape mixture into walnut-size balls.
- Roll dough gently with palm of hand from left to right until dough is about 4 inches in length.
- Connect both ends of each dough strand to form a ring.
- Put a pistachio nut or almond on the seam of each ring.
- Bake at 350°F for 10 minutes. Should remain white when finished baking.
- Cool completely before removing from the tray.

CHEESE DANISH

So much better than store-bought Danish. Serve warm or cold.

Dough
½ lb. cream cheese
½ lb. sweet butter
2 cups flour
1 egg yolk

Filling
1 lb. farmer cheese
½ lb. cream cheese
1 cup sugar
1 egg
1 tsp. vanilla extract
1 Tbsp. flour

Yields 10 slices per loaf.

- Mix dough ingredients in a food processor or mixer until mixture forms a ball of dough.
- Divide dough into 2 equal parts. Set aside.
- In a bowl, mix filling ingredients, blending well.
- Roll out 1 portion of dough into a 12 by 16-inch rectangle.
- Fill center of rectangle with half of filling.
- Fold dough to center, overlapping both sides and then both ends of the dough.
- Make a 3-inch slit down the center of the dough.
- Repeat entire process for second portion of dough.
- Place Danish on a greased cookie sheet, and freeze for several hours.
- Remove from freezer, and bake seam side down at 350°F for 45 to 50 minutes.
- Optional: Brush tops of Danish with apricot jam before baking. Sprinkle with powdered sugar after baking.

CRUMB CAKE

This is a crumb cake that truly lives up to its name.

3 cups flour
1½ cups sugar
5 Tbsps. baking powder
1½ tsps. salt
½ cup butter or margarine
1½ cups milk or non-dairy substitute
2 eggs

<u>Topping</u>
3 cups flour
¾ cup sugar
1½ Tbsps. cinnamon
1½ cups butter or margarine
confectioners' sugar

Yields 20 servings.

- Combine dry ingredients.
- In a mixer, beat remaining cake ingredients. Add dry ingredients and mix well.
- Pour batter into a greased jelly roll pan.
- Bake at 350°F for 20 minutes.
- While cake is baking, mix flour, sugar, and cinnamon.
- Cut butter or margarine into small pieces, and work by hand into flour mixture until it is well blended and has a crumby consistency.
- Remove cake from oven and sprinkle crumb mixture on top, pressing down lightly.
- Bake for an additional 20 minutes.
- Let cake cool for 1 hour and sprinkle confectioners' sugar on top.

CARAMEL CUSTARD FLAN

This recipe from the New York Times *is Craig Clayborn's finest. Pure and simple to prepare.*

⅔ cup sugar
¼ cup water
2½ cups milk
1 cup heavy cream
4 whole eggs
4 egg yolks
⅓ cup sugar
⅛ tsp. salt
1 tsp. vanilla extract

Yields 8–10 servings.

- *Carmelize the sugar: Put sugar and water in a saucepan. Do not stir. Bring mixture to a boil, swirling the pot until sugar is dissolved. Continue boiling, swirling the saucepan frequently until liquid is caramel colored.*
- *As soon as sugar is caramelized, pour it into a 1½-quart ring mold, tilting the mold so the inside surface is completely covered with caramel. Let cool.*
- *While the caramelized sugar is cooling, combine and scald the milk and cream.*
- *In a bowl, blend remaining ingredients.*
- *Add milk mixture to egg mixture and blend well.*
- *Pour mixture over cooled caramelized sugar.*
- *Place mold in a shallow pan containing boiling water, and bake at 325°F for 45 minutes.*
- *Let cool completely and refrigerate.*

CHOCOLATE CHIP COOKIES

The extra walnuts in these cookies make them high and fabulous.

½ cup butter or margarine
⅓ cup sugar
⅓ cup brown sugar
1 egg
½ tsp. vanilla extract
1 cup plus 2 Tbsps. flour
½ tsp. baking powder
½ tsp. salt
1 cup chocolate chips
2 cups whole walnuts

Yields 25–30 cookies.

- *Cream butter or margarine and sugars in a mixer.*
- *Add egg and vanilla, and mix.*
- *Combine flour, baking powder, and salt.*
- *Slowly add flour mixture to sugar mixture, and blend. Do not overblend.*
- *Add chocolate chips and walnuts, and mix gently.*
- *Spoon heaping tablespoons of dough onto an ungreased cookie sheet, spacing dough 1½ inches apart.*
- *Bake at mid-level in oven at 375°F for 15 minutes.*
- *When cookies are done, immediately loosen cookies from tray with spatula, and let cool.*

CARROT CAKE

This was my sister-in-law's recipe. The secret ingredient is the pineapple, which gives the cake a moist texture.

1½ cups flour
1 tsp. baking powder
1 tsp. baking soda
⅓ tsp. salt
1 cup sugar
1 tsp. cinnamon
⅔ cup oil
2 eggs
½ cup crushed pineapple, drained
1 cup grated carrots

Yields 8 servings.

- *Combine first 6 ingredients in a mixer.*
- *Add remaining ingredients to dry ingredients, and combine.*
- *Pour batter into a greased and floured 10-inch tube pan.*
- *Bake at 350°F for 35 minutes or until brown.*

DATE CAKES

A pleasant finger cake to have with your coffee or tea.

<u>Dough</u>
3 cups flour
1 cup butter or margarine, room temperature
½ cup water

<u>Filling</u>
1 lb. pitted dates, cut into small pieces (hint: cut dates with a wet scissors)
1 cup water
1 Tbsp. butter or margarine
1 tsp. orange rind
¼ tsp. cinnamon
½ cup chopped walnuts
confectioners' sugar

Yields 60 miniature cakes.

- Thoroughly mix flour and butter or margarine in a mixer or food processor.
- Add water to flour mixture until it forms a ball of dough. Set aside.
- In a covered saucepan, cook dates in water for 15 minutes until soft.
- Add butter or margarine, orange rind, cinnamon, and walnuts to dates, and mix.
- Let date mixture cool.
- Shape dough into walnut-size balls, and roll out to make 3-inch circles (or use a tortilla press).
- Place 1 teaspoon of the date mixture in the center of each circle.
- Roll up each circle into a log, and bend to form a crescent shape.
- Bake on an ungreased cookie sheet at 350°F for 15 to 20 minutes.
- Let cakes cool, and sprinkle with confectioners' sugar.
- May be frozen before or after baking.

GRAHAM CRACKER ROLL

Similar to a fruit cake and easy to slice — as good as candy.

1 lb. ground graham crackers
7 oz. miniature marshmallows
1 lb. chopped dates
1 lb. chopped figs
½ lb. chopped walnuts
2 oz. evaporated milk

Yields 30–40 slices.

- Reserve 1 cup ground graham crackers.
- Thoroughly mix together all remaining ingredients.
- Shape mixture into 2 rolls, and roll each in reserved graham cracker crumbs.
- Wrap each roll in aluminum foil and refrigerate until ready to serve.
- Cut each roll into ¼-inch slices immediately before serving.

COCONUT CANDY

You're in for a really different treat.

½ cup butter
1½ cups graham cracker crumbs
14 oz. condensed milk
6 oz. chocolate chips
1⅓ cups flaked coconut
1 cup chopped walnuts

Yields 30 squares.

- Melt butter, and pour into a 3-quart casserole.
- Evenly sprinkle graham cracker crumbs over butter.
- Pour milk over crumbs.
- Top with a layer of chocolate chips, a layer of coconut, and then a layer of walnuts.
- Bake at 325°F for 25 to 30 minutes until lightly browned. Cool, and cut into squares.
- Can be frozen.

HAMANTASHEN

The combination of the fruit butter and the dried fruits thickens the filling. Very light due to a thin dough which makes it easy to eat more than one.

¾ cup oil
2 eggs, beaten
1 cup sugar
1 tsp. vanilla extract
⅓ cup orange juice
4 cups flour
½ tsp. salt
3 tsps. baking powder
32 oz. prune butter
12 pitted prunes
24 oz. apricot butter
10 dried apricots

Yields 50 to 60.

- Cream oil, eggs, and sugar in a mixer. Add vanilla.
- Combine dry ingredients, and add alternately with orange juice to egg mixture.
- Blend prunes and prune butter in blender until a smooth paste is formed. Set aside.
- Blend apricots and apricot butter in blender until a smooth paste is formed.
- Roll out dough as thin as possible on a floured board.
- Cut dough into 3-inch rounds.
- Put 1 teaspoon of either prune or apricot filling in middle of each round.
- Pinch 3 sides together to form a triangle shape.
- Bake at 350°F for 20 minutes.

KANAFE
(Shredded Dough)

This is the real thing. A traditional, deliciously rich dessert.

⅔ cup milk
1 cup heavy cream
2 Tbsps. sugar
2 Tbsps. cornstarch
2 lbs. ricotta cheese
1 lb. Kanafe
1½ cups butter

<u>Syrup</u>
1 cup water
2 cups sugar
1 tsp. lemon juice
1 tsp. orange water

Yields 8–10 servings.

- Mix milk, cream, sugar, and cornstarch in a saucepan.
- Bring mixture to a boil until it thickens. Remove from heat.
- When mixture is completely cooled, blend with ricotta cheese.
- Separate all strands of the Kanafe until dough is completely shredded.
- Melt butter and pour over Kanafe.
- With both hands work butter into Kanafe until dough is completely coated.
- Spread half of Kanafe on bottom of a 3-quart casserole, flattening evenly with the palm of your hand.
- Spread ricotta mixture over Kanafe.
- Top with remaining Kanafe. Do not press. At this point can be frozen.
- Bake Kanafe on the day it will be served. Bake at 350°F for 1 hour or until golden brown. If frozen, bake for 1 hour and 15 minutes.
- Make sugar syrup as instructed on page 161.
- Let syrup cool. As soon as Kanafe is removed from oven, pour cold syrup evenly over entire Kanafe.

KANAFE RING

The exquisite taste of Kanafe with a light touch so you don't feel like you're overindulging.

1 lb. Kanafe
4 cups ricotta cheese
1 cup sweet butter, melted and cooled

<u>Syrup</u>
1 cup water
2 cups sugar
1 tsp. fresh lemon juice
1 tsp. orange water

Yields 12–15 servings.

- Unwind Kanafe and cut in half. Put one half back in the box, wrapped well, and freeze for later use.
- Cut remainder of Kanafe in half lengthwise, and cut each of these pieces into thirds, so that you have six 8-inch strips.
- On wax paper, spread out each strip widthwise to a 6-inch width.
- Add 2 heaping tablespoons of ricotta cheese to one of the 6-inch long sides of Kanafe and spread cheese along the edge.
- Pick up edge of Kanafe containing the cheese and roll until Kanafe is all rolled up. Repeat for remaining strips of dough.
- In a greased glass 9-inch pie plate arrange the rolls first around the perimeter, working inward toward the center.
- Pour cooled butter evenly over top. Kanafe may be frozen at this point.
- On the day it will be served, bake at 350°F for 35 to 40 minutes.
- **To prepare syrup:** Bring water, sugar, and lemon juice to a boil. Boil for 4 minutes.
- Add orange water, and stir well.
- Chill syrup and pour over hot Kanafe.
- Syrup can be stored in refrigerator.

KA'AK-IB-LOZ
(Almond-Pistachio Rings)

Very pretty. Served mainly at a bridal table, but special for any occasion.

1 cup almonds
1 cup pistachio nuts
1 cup confectioners' sugar
1 Tbsp. orange water
6 to 8 drops green food coloring

Yields 10–14 rings.

- Blanch, shell, and thoroughly dry nuts.
- Grind nuts in a food processor until pulverized.
- Add sugar to nuts, and process for an additional 10 seconds.
- Put orange water and food coloring in a bowl, and blend well. (If pistachios are a deep green eliminate the coloring.)
- Add ground nuts to orange water, and mix well until mixture becomes an even green.
- Shape mixture into walnut-size balls.
- Roll out each ball and join ends to make a ring.
- Place rings on wax paper and leave out overnight to dry.
- Use a strawberry husker to make small pinches in the dough.
- May be frozen.

SWEET KA'AK
(Crackers)

Not too sweet and a great nosh.

3 eggs
¾ cup sugar
1 cup oil
¼ tsp. orange extract
½ tsp. vanilla extract
½ tsp. lemon or orange rind
3 cups flour
1½ tsps. baking powder
4 Tbsps. apricot preserves
2 Tbsps. water

Yields 60 cookies.

- *Beat eggs and sugar in a mixer until creamy.*
- *Add oil, orange extract, vanilla, and rind to egg mixture. Beat well.*
- *Gradually add flour and baking powder to egg mixture, mixing by hand a little at a time.*
- *Shape mixture into walnut-size balls.*
- *Roll each ball into a 4-inch-long twisted rope, and place on an ungreased cookie sheet.*
- *Mix apricot preserves with water.*
- *Heat and strain.*
- *Brush preserves on cookies, and bake at 350°F for 30 to 35 minutes or until golden brown.*

KRABEEG
(Marshmallow Fluff Cookies)

As a child, I considered this one of my favorites. A dab of marshmallow enhances the taste and appearance of this cookie.

2 cups flour
1 cup semolina
1 cup butter or margarine
½ cup water
1 lb. chopped walnuts
¼ cup sugar
1 tsp. cinnamon
2 Tbsps. butter or margarine
1 tsp. orange water
marshmallow fluff

Yields 60 cookies.

- Mix flour, semolina, and butter or margarine in a mixer or food processor.
- Add water to mixture, and beat until it forms dough.
- Form the dough into walnut-size balls. Shape each ball into a cup shape.
- Mix walnuts, sugar, cinnamon, butter or margarine, and orange water.
- Fill each cup with 1 teaspoon of nut mixture.
- Close up each cup to form an oval shape.
- Place cookies on a cookie sheet, and bake at 400°F for 15 minutes.
- When cookies have cooled, top each one with 1 teaspoon of marshmallow fluff.
- May be frozen before or after baking.

LEMON MERINGUE PIE

As a young girl, lemon meringue pie was one of my favorites. As an adult, I searched until I found a recipe that withstands the test of my memories.

<u>Piecrust</u>
1 cup flour
⅓ cup solid shortening
pinch of salt
¼ cup ice water

<u>Filling</u>
1¼ cups sugar
⅓ cup cornstarch
½ tsp. salt
1½ cups cold water
3 egg yolks
2 Tbsps. margarine
1 Tbsp. grated lemon peel
⅓ cup fresh lemon juice

<u>Meringue</u>
4 egg whites
½ tsp. vanilla extract
6 Tbsps. sugar

Yields 8 servings.

- Mix flour, shortening, and salt in a food processor.
- Gradually add water to flour mixture, mixing until a ball of dough is formed.
- Roll out dough and place in a 9-inch pie plate.
- Bake at 400°F for 15 minutes or until lightly browned. Cool.
- In a medium saucepan, combine 1¼ cups sugar, cornstarch, and salt, mixing well.
- Gradually stir in cold water until sugar mixture is smooth.
- Cook over medium heat, stirring constantly, until mixture boils. Boil for one minute, continuing to stir. Remove from heat.
- In a small bowl, beat egg yolks, then stir about ¼ cup of hot sugar mixture into egg yolks. Gradually stir yolk mixture into remaining hot sugar mixture. Cook over low heat, stirring constantly, until mixture boils.
- Boil mixture for one minute, stirring constantly.
- Remove saucepan from heat. Stir in margarine, lemon peel, and lemon juice.
- Cool slightly, about 15 minutes. Pour mixture into cooled, baked pie shell.

(recipe continued next page)

- *Beat egg whites and vanilla at medium speed until soft peaks form.*
- *Add sugar very gradually, beating at high speed, until stiff, glossy peaks form.*
- *Spoon meringue over filling; spread to edge of crust to seal well and prevent shrinkage.*
- *Bake at 350°F for 12 to 15 minutes or until light golden brown. Cool completely. Refrigerate for 3 hours or until filling is set.*

HEAVENLY HASH

No wonder it's called heavenly. What's not to love with these delicious ingredients? Fun to make with kids.

32 oz. chocolate
7 oz. large marshmallows
1 cup walnuts (large pieces)

Yields 20 to 30 pieces.

- *Break chocolate into chunks, and place in top part of a double boiler.*
- *Stir chocolate often until melted and smooth. (Chocolate can also be melted by microwaving for 1 minute.)*
- *Using a fork, dip 1 marshmallow into melted chocolate, and place in a bowl.*
- *Repeat process for remaining marshmallows.*
- *Add walnuts, mix, and shape mixture into a mound.*
- *Refrigerate for one day.*
- *When ready to serve, slice, then cut each slice into 1½-inch pieces.*

MAMOULE
(Nut-Filled Cookies)

A variation of Krabeeg but round in shape. Allow for artistic expression. Have fun.

Dough
2 cups flour
1 cup semolina
1 cup butter or margarine, room temperature
½ cup water

Filling
1 lb. chopped walnuts or pistachio nuts
½ cup sugar
1 tsp. cinnamon
1 tsp. orange water
2 Tbsps. butter or margarine, melted
confectioners' sugar

Yields 60 cookies.

- *Mix flour, semolina, and butter or margarine in a mixer or food processor.*
- *Add water to flour mixture, and continue mixing until it forms a ball of dough. Set aside.*
- *In a bowl, mix chopped nuts, sugar, cinnamon, orange water, and melted butter or margarine.*
- *Shape dough into walnut-size balls, and then into a cup shape.*
- *Fill each cup with 1 teaspoon nut mixture.*
- *Close up each cup, and shape into a ball.*
- *Make a design on top of each ball with a strawberry husker. Cookies may be frozen at this point.*
- *Bake at 400°F for 15 minutes. If frozen, bake for 20 minutes.*
- *Sprinkle cookies with confectioners' sugar.*

ORANGE CRÊPES

When I was engaged my husband sent me to cooking school where I learned how to section oranges for this recipe. It looks difficult, which makes me look great.

<u>Dessert Crêpes</u>
2 eggs
¾ cup flour
2 Tbsps. sugar
1 cup milk or non-dairy creamer
1 Tbsp. brandy
1 Tbsp. butter or margarine, melted and cooled

<u>Filling</u>
8 large oranges
grated rind and juice of 1 fresh lemon
grated rind and juice of 2 oranges
¾ cup sugar
2 Tbsps. cornstarch
2 Tbsps. margarine or butter
oil or cooking spray

Yields 20–30 crêpes.

- Mix eggs, flour, sugar, milk or non-dairy creamer, brandy, and margarine in blender. Set aside for 1 hour.
- Peel oranges, removing white outer membrane.
- With a sharp paring knife, remove orange sections between membranes.
- Combine lemon rind, lemon juice, orange rind, orange juice, sugar, and cornstarch.
- Cook mixture over low heat, stirring constantly until it thickens.
- Add orange sections and butter or margarine, and cook until heated through. Cool.
- Pour 1 tablespoon crêpe batter into a 4-inch, lightly greased skillet, tilting the pan so that batter covers the bottom and sides.
- Cook on a low heat for 30 to 40 seconds on one side and 15 to 20 seconds on the other side. Remove from skillet, and repeat process for remainder of batter.
- Fill each crêpe with 3 or 4 orange sections.
- Place crêpes into a greased casserole, and pour remaining sauce on top.
- Bake at 400°F for 15 minutes.

DESSERTS

ORANGE FANTASIA

Your guests will be most impressed with this juicy and elegant dessert.

8 oranges
2 cups sugar
1 cup water
1 tsp. lemon juice
4 Tbsps. orange liqueur
cooking spray

Yields 14–16 servings.

- *Remove zest (the outer peel of the orange) from oranges with a vegetable peeler, taking care not to remove white pith.*
- *Slice zest into julienne strips.*
- *With a sharp knife, remove any remaining peel and the pith from oranges.*
- *Cut oranges crosswise into ½-inch-thick slices.*
- *Combine sugar, water, and lemon juice in a saucepan.*
- *Bring mixture to a boil, and boil for 5 minutes. Remove from heat and cool.*
- *Arrange orange slices on a plate, and add ½ cup cooled syrup and liqueur to orange slices.*
- *Spray cooking spray on a baking sheet.*
- *Reheat remaining syrup, bringing it to a boil.*
- *Add orange zests to syrup and let boil slowly for 5 minutes.*
- *Remove zests from saucepan with a slotted spoon, and spread on a baking sheet to cool.*
- *Sprinkle candied zests on top of orange slices. Serve chilled.*

PASSOVER NUT CAKE

A Passover favorite. You won't miss bread during the holiday.

12 large eggs, separated
1½ cups sifted sugar
½ cup orange juice
1 cup ground walnuts
1 cup cake meal, sifted
2 heaping tsps. potato starch, sifted

Yields 8–10 servings.

- *Beat egg yolks, adding sugar gradually until creamy and pale yellow.*
- *Add orange juice and nuts to egg yolk mixture, mixing after the addition of each.*
- *Beat egg whites until very stiff.*
- *Add cake meal and potato starch to yolk mixture, and beat well. Fold in egg whites.*
- *Place batter in a well-greased 10-inch tube pan and bake at 350°F for 70 minutes.*
- *Allow cake to cool completely before removing from pan.*

TROPICAL FRUIT SALAD

An exotic way to serve fruits that are in season.

1 mango
1 kiwi
1 banana
1 orange
10 strawberries
juice of ½ lemon

Yields 3 to 4 servings.

- *Cut mango and kiwi into cubes.*
- *Slice banana.*
- *Slice orange into wedges.*
- *Slice strawberries.*
- *Combine fruit in a bowl, and squeeze lemon juice over fruit.*
- *Refrigerate.*

DEEP DISH PEACH PIE

This is a real peachy pie with a crisp topping. A perfect summer treat.

Piecrust
1½ cups flour
1½ Tbsps. sugar
½ tsp. salt
½ cup butter or margarine
1 egg yolk
4–5 Tbsps. ice water

Filling
7 cups fresh, sliced peaches
2 Tbsps. fresh lemon juice
½ cup sugar
¼ cup flour

Topping
1 cup flour
¾ cup brown sugar
1 tsp. cinnamon
¼ tsp. salt
½ cup butter or margarine, cut into small pieces

Yields 6–8 servings.

- *Combine flour, sugar, and salt.*
- *Add butter or margarine, and work into flour mixture with your hands or a pastry cutter until it resembles cornmeal.*
- *Add egg yolk and ice water, blending well until mixture forms a ball of dough.*
- *Wrap dough in plastic, and refrigerate for 30 minutes.*
- *On a floured board, roll out dough to a ⅛-inch thickness and place in a 10-inch, deep dish pie pan.*
- *Place aluminum foil on top of dough and fill with pie weights or 1 cup dried beans to weigh down crust.*
- *Bake pie crust at 425°F for 10 minutes. Lower heat to 375°F, and bake for an additional 5 minutes, until crust is lightly browned.*
- *Place peaches in a large bowl and toss with lemon juice.*
- *Add sugar and flour to peaches, coating well.*
- *Combine first 4 topping ingredients.*
- *Work butter or margarine into topping mixture with your fingers until well mixed.*
- *Place filling into pie shell and cover with topping.*
- *Bake at 375°F for 30 to 40 minutes. Serve warm.*

PECAN PIE

This pie contains many more pecans than most pecan pies. When you taste it you'll know it was worth the time and effort.

Piecrust
1½ cups flour
½ cup solid shortening or margarine
¼ cup ice water

Filling
3 eggs
⅔ cup sugar
dash of salt
½ cup light corn syrup
½ cup dark corn syrup
1 tsp. vanilla extract
½ cup butter or margarine, melted
2 cups chopped pecans
36 whole pecans

Yields 2 pies.

- Mix flour and shortening or margarine in a food processor.
- Add water, mixing until it forms a ball of dough.
- Divide dough in half.
- Roll out each half into a circle on a well-floured board, and place each circle in a 9-inch pie pan.
- Beat eggs well in a mixer.
- Add sugar and salt, and blend well.
- Add syrups, vanilla, and butter or margarine to egg mixture, and mix.
- Add chopped pecans to mixture, and mix.
- Pour mixture into the piecrusts and arrange whole pecans on top.
- Bake at 350°F for 1 hour.
- May be frozen.

PINEAPPLE NUT CAKE

The fruit and nuts make this cake really chewy. The topping adds zest.

<u>Cake</u>

2 eggs

2 cups sugar

1 tsp. vanilla extract

2 cups flour

2 tsps. baking soda

1 cup canned, crushed pineapple, drained

1 cup chopped walnuts or pecans

<u>Topping</u>

8 oz. cream cheese

½ cup margarine or butter

1½ cups confectioners' sugar

1 tsp. vanilla extract

Yields 8–10 servings.

- *Beat eggs, add sugar gradually, and add vanilla, mixing until creamy.*
- *Add flour, baking soda, pineapple, and nuts.*
- *Pour into a greased and floured 10-inch springform pan.*
- *Bake at 350°F for 50 to 60 minutes.*
- *Mix cream cheese and margarine or butter well.*
- *Gradually add confectioners' sugar and vanilla while mixing. Chill for at least half an hour.*
- *Spread topping on cake as frosting.*

PASSOVER PISTACHIO COOKIES

Perfect for Passover, but just as enjoyable all year round. Be prepared for many recipe requests.

3 cups shelled pistachio nuts

3 egg whites

1 cup sugar

confectioners' sugar

Yields 24 cookies.

- *Process the nuts in a food processor until coarsely chopped. Some nuts should remain whole.*
- *Line cookie sheets with parchment paper and set aside.*
- *Beat the egg whites until frothy.*
- *In a bowl, mix the nuts, egg whites, and sugar until well incorporated.*
- *Refrigerate mixture for 10 minutes.*
- *Drop heaping teaspoons of the batter onto the cookie sheets, leaving about 1 inch between each.*
- *Bake at 350°F for 12 to 15 minutes or until lightly browned, and remove from oven.*
- *Allow about 5 minutes to cool, and very carefully remove cookies from cookie sheets with a spatula.*
- *When completely cooled, dust with confectioners' sugar.*

DESSERTS

RICE PUDDING

This is special. Has a most pleasant taste with the lemon zest.

3 cups water
1 cup rice
zest of two lemons
2 cinnamon sticks
6 cups milk
1½ cups sugar

Yields 10 to 12 servings.

- Bring water to a boil, and add rice, lemon zest, and cinnamon sticks.
- Cook rice on medium flame for about 15 minutes, until water is almost completely absorbed.
- Add milk and sugar to mixture and stir.
- When mixture thickens, simmer, covered, for 1½ hours.
- Remove zest and cinnamon sticks after cooking.

MIXED BERRIES SALAD

In season, serve often. A refreshing mixture of berries.

1 cup blueberries
1 cup raspberries
1 cup sliced strawberries
2 Tbsps. fresh lemon juice
2½ Tbsps. sugar
8–10 fresh, chopped mint leaves

Yields 6–8 servings.

- Clean, rinse, and drain all berries.
- Dry berries on a paper towel, and then combine.
- Add lemon juice, sugar, and mint to berries.
- Refrigerate for 1 hour before serving.
- Optional: Add 2 tablespoons brandy.

DAIRY RUGELACH

Rugelach should only be made with this wonderful dough. So light and creamy.

½ lb. cream cheese, room temperature
½ lb. butter, room temperature
2 cups flour
½ cup sugar

<u>Filling</u>

8 oz. preserves
1 cup chopped walnuts
½ cup raisins
sugar and cinnamon for sprinkling

Yields 25–30 rugelach.

- *Beat cream cheese and butter together in a mixer until smooth.*
- *Add flour and sugar to cheese mixture and mix well.*
- *Refrigerate dough overnight.*
- *Let dough warm at room temperature for 30 minutes before working with it.*
- *Roll a golf ball size ball of dough into a flat circle.*
- *Divide into 4 or 6 triangles.*
- *Spread some preserves, nuts, and 5 or 6 raisins on each triangle, so that the filling covers the entire surface.*
- *Roll up each triangle, starting at wide base and rolling toward the point.*
- *Place rugelach on a cookie sheet with the pointed ends facing down.*
- *Sprinkle with sugar and cinnamon, and bake at 350°F for 20 to 25 minutes or until golden brown.*

STRAWBERRY SHORTCAKE

A must for birthday or dinner parties.

¾ cup margarine or shortening
1½ cup sugar
1½ tsp. vanilla
2¼ cups flour
3 tsps. baking powder
1 tsp. salt
1 cup milk or non-dairy substitute
5 egg whites

4 cups strawberries
2 Tbsps. sugar
1 cup pareve whipped topping or heavy cream

- *Cream margarine or shortening and sugar until light and fluffy. Add vanilla.*
- *Sift together flour, baking powder, and salt.*
- *Add milk or non-dairy substitute alternately with flour mixture to creamed margarine and sugar, then beat with electric mixer for two minutes at medium speed.*
- *Beat egg whites until stiff, and fold into batter.*
- *Bake in 2 greased and floured 9-inch cake pans at 375°F for 20 minutes.*
- *Cool for 10 minutes before removing from pan.*
- *Wash, hull, and dry strawberries. Separate the largest strawberries for the top of the cake.*
- *Slice remaining strawberries. Sprinkle with sugar and let stand for 30 minutes.*
- *Whip pareve topping or cream until it forms stiff peaks.*
- *Split one 9-inch cake layer in half to form two thin layers. (Freeze the other cake for another time.)*
- *Spread cream on the bottom layer, and place sliced strawberries on the cream.*
- *Put the second layer on top of strawberries and cream, and spread cream over the top and sides.*
- *Cover top of cake with whole strawberries, and refrigerate until ready to serve.*

SUTTLAGE FINGERS
(Cornstarch Pudding Pastries)

A delicate and light phyllo dessert.

4 cups milk
½ cup cornstarch
3 Tbsps. sugar
1 tsp. orange water
1 lb. phyllo dough
1 cup butter, clarified (see Food Prep. Tips, p. 15)
sugar and cinnamon for sprinkling

Yields 40.

- *Combine milk, cornstarch, and sugar in a saucepan, and bring to a boil.*
- *Reduce heat and stir mixture constantly for about 15 minutes until it thickens.*
- *Transfer mixture from saucepan to bowl, stir in orange water, and pour into a 15½ x 10½ x 1-inch baking tray.*
- *Cool thoroughly. Refrigerate until firm.*
- *Slice pudding into 2 x 1-inch bars.*
- *Cut phyllo lengthwise into 2 halves measuring 6 by 17 inches each.*
- *Keeping unused phyllo covered, take 2 strips of phyllo and lay them one on top of the other.*
- *Brush uppermost strip with butter, and place 1 pudding bar at bottom of phyllo strip.*
- *Fold the bottom edge of filo over pudding.*
- *Fold in left side and right side. Brush sides with butter.*
- *Roll up pastry to end.*
- *Sprinkle with sugar and cinnamon.*
- *Repeat procedure for remainder of pudding and phyllo strips.*
- *Bake at 350°F for 20 minutes.*

SPONGE CAKE

A Passover must. And delicious any time.

8 extra large eggs, separated
1½ cups sifted sugar
2 Tbsps. lemon juice
2 tsps. lemon rind
¾ cup potato starch
¼ tsp. salt

Yields 8–10 servings.

- *Beat egg yolks well, add sugar gradually, and continue beating until yolks are very light in color.*
- *Add lemon juice, rind, potato starch, and salt.*
- *In a separate bowl, beat egg whites until stiff.*
- *Fold whites into yolk mixture.*
- *Pour batter into an ungreased tube pan and bake at 350°F for 70 minutes.*
- *Remove from oven and invert immediately. Cool completely, then use a sharp knife to loosen edges from sides of pan.*
- *May be used for Passover.*

STRAWBERRY COMPOTE

Served on ice cream or pound cake, strawberries with sauce are luscious.

4 cups fresh whole strawberries
10 oz. frozen raspberries, thawed
3 Tbsps. confectioners' sugar
2 Tbsps. orange brandy

Yields 6–8 servings.

- *Wash and hull strawberries.*
- *Mix frozen raspberries with sugar and brandy in a food processor.*
- *Strain raspberries, discard the pulp, and add sauce to strawberries.*
- *Delicious with ice cream or sherbet.*
- *May be prepared a few hours before serving.*

THUMBPRINT COOKIES

My grandchildren love putting the jelly in the center of the cookie.

½ cup butter or margarine

¼ cup firmly packed brown sugar

1 egg, separated

½ tsp. vanilla extract

1 cup flour

¼ tsp. salt

1 cup walnuts, finely chopped

jelly or marmalade

Yields 25 cookies.

- *Cream butter or margarine, sugar, egg yolk, and vanilla in a mixer.*
- *Combine flour and salt.*
- *Add flour mixture to butter mixture and mix gently and thoroughly by hand.*
- *Beat egg white slightly.*
- *Shape dough into balls, using 1 teaspoon of dough for each.*
- *Dip each ball into egg white, then into chopped nuts.*
- *Shape each ball into a round, make a depression in the center with thumb, and add a small amount of jelly or marmalade in the center.*
- *Bake cookies on an ungreased cookie sheet at 350°F for 12 to 15 minutes.*

FRUIT TART

Can be made with peaches or pears. I tried them both and they are equally tasty.

Crust
1¾ cups flour
½ cup sugar
⅛ tsp. salt
2 egg yolks (reserve egg whites)
½ cup sweet butter or margarine, room temperature, cut into small pieces
½ tsp. lemon rind
water, if needed

Glaze
1 cup apricot preserves
2 Tbsps. cornstarch
2 Tbsps. sugar
23 oz. canned apricot halves, drained

Yields 10 servings.

- **To make crust:** Combine flour, sugar, and salt in a bowl.
- *Make a well in center.*
- *Add egg yolks, butter or margarine, and lemon rind to well, mixing just enough to combine.*
- *If mixture is dry add 1 tablespoon water.*
- *Shape dough into a flat round, and chill for 1 hour.*
- *Press dough into a 2-piece tart pan (a shallow, fluted-edged pan whose bottom is removed after baking), pressing edges so they are not too thick.*
- *Brush crust with egg white and bake at 350°F for 15 minutes.*
- **To make glaze:** *Heat preserves.*
- *Mix sugar and cornstarch, and add to preserves.*
- *Boil mixture until thick.*
- *Remove from stove.*
- *Arrange apricot halves on crust close together, pressing them firmly into crust.*
- *Spoon warm glaze over fruit.*
- *Bake at 375°F for 12 to 15 minutes.*
- *Place on a rack for 15 minutes and let cool.*
- *Place pan on coffee can and push side ring to remove.*

EQUIVALENTS

3 teaspoons = 1 tablespoon
4 tablespoons = ¼ cup
8 tablespoons = ½ cup
16 tablespoons = 1 cup
2 cups = 1 pint
4 cups = 1 quart
4 quarts = 1 gallon

Butter or margarine: 1 stick = ½ cup; 2 cups = 1 pound
Chocolate chips: 1 cup = 6 oz.
Graham crackers (crushed) 16 squares = 1¼ cups
All-purpose flour: 3½ cups = 1 pound
Granulated sugar: 4 cups = 1 pound
Shelled walnuts: 4 cups = 1 pound
Lemon juice: 1 medium lemon = 3 tablespoons

GLOSSARY

Almasyia — Cornstarch pudding
Ataiyef — Stuffed pancakes
Baba Ghanouj — Eggplant and tahini salad
Baklava — Phyllo dough filled with nuts
Bedab Lemuna — Egg and lemon sauce
Bestell — Dough filled with meat
Bizzard — Roasted pumpkin seeds
Bulgur — Cracked wheat salad
Jibbon — Vegetable, egg, and cheese mixture
Kanafe — Shredded dough
Keftes — Meatball sauce
Kelsonaise — Cheese ravioli
Kibbe Homda — Sour sauce
Kibbe or Torpedoes — Cracked wheat casing filled with meat
Kibbe Neye (pareve) — Combination of cracked wheat and vegetables
Krabeeg — Marshmallow fluff cookie
Krefsiah — Swiss chard
Lahemageen — Dough patty with meat
Lubyeh — Black-eyed peas
Mamoule — Nut-filled cookies
Medias — Stuffed artichokes
Mechshe — Stuffed vegetables
M'gedrah — Lentils and rice

Sambousak — Dough filled with cheese
Salata — Chopped Syrian Salad
Sul Ajon — Ground meat on a skewer
Suttlage — Cornstarch fingers
Tahini — Sesame paste
Tabouli — Vegetables and cracked wheat

INDEX

A
Ades (Red Lentil Soup) 52
Almasyia (Cornstarch Pudding) 145
APPETIZERS
  Baba Ghanouj (Eggplant and Tahini Salad) 23
  Bazaghan (Cracked Wheat Salad) 20
  Bestell (Meat-Filled Dough) 21
  Blehat (Meat Stuffed with Egg) 19
  Cheddar-Cheese Balls 24
  Chicken in Phyllo 22
  Eggplant Salad 25
  Egg Rolls 26
  Empanadas 27
  Kibbe Matzah (with Fish Filling for Pesach) 30
  Kibbe Neye 37
  Kibbe Torpedoes 29
  Kibbe with Vegetable Filling 31
  Lahemageen (Meat Pizza) 32
  Mushroom Turnovers 33
  Pickles — Artichokes and Mushrooms 34
  Pickles — Carrots and Green Pepper 35
  Pickles — Cauliflower, Cabbage, and Turnips 36
  Potato Knishes in Phyllo 28
  Sambousak (Cheese-and-Egg-Filled Dough) 39
  Spinach Phyllo 38
  Tahini Dip 40
APPLES
  Apple Crisp 142
  Apple Pie 141
Apricot Candy 144
Apricot-Prune Chicken 112
ARTICHOKES
  Artichoke Medias (Stuffed Artichoke Hearts) 71
  Artichokes in Oil 72
  Pickled Artichokes 34
Asparagus Winter 72
Ataiyef (Stuffed Pancakes) 143

B
Baba Ghanouj (Eggplant and Tahini Salad) 23
Baked Fried Potatoes 80
Baked Shells in Tomato Sauce 133
Baked Whitefish 117
Baklava 147
Basic Crêpes 123
Basil Sauce, Fresh (for Pasta) 60
Bazaghan (Cracked Wheat Salad) 20
BEANS
  Fava Bean Salad 43
  Great Northern Beans 73
  Lubyeh (Black-Eyed Peas) 76

Bedab Lemuna (Lemon Sauce) 62
Beef — see Meat
Beef Stroganoff 85
Bestell (Meat-Filled Dough) 21
Bizzard (Roasted Pumpkin Seeds) 148
Blehat (Meat Stuffed with Egg) 19
Blintz Soufflé 121
Blueberry Muffins 146
Bread Pudding 145
Broccoli and Cauliflower, Creamed 75
Broiled Fillet of Sole 116
Broiled Salmon 117
Bulgur with Cheese 121
Butter — *to clarify margarine or butter* 15

C

CABBAGE
  Pickled Cabbage 36
  Pickled Corned Beef and Cabbage 88
  Stuffed Cabbage 87
Caesar Salad 43
CAKE
  Carrot Cake 156
  Cheese Danish 152
  Cream Cheese Cake 151
  Crumb Cake 153
  Date and Nut Bread 148
  Graham Cracker Roll 158
  Kanafe (Shredded Dough) 160
  Kanafe Ring 161
  Passover Nut Cake 170
  Pineapple Nut Cake 173
  Sponge Cake 179
  Strawberry Shortcake 177
Cauliflower and Broccoli, Creamed 75
CANDY
  Apricot Candy 144
  Coconut Candy 158
  Heavenly Hash 166

Caramel Custard Flan 154
CARROTS
  Baked Carrots 73
  Carrot Cake 156
  Carrot Ring 74
  Pickled Carrots 35
Cheese — see also Dairy Dishes
CHEESE
  Bulgur with Cheese 121
  Cheddar-Cheese Balls 24
  Cheese Danish 152
  Cream Cheese Cake 151
  Eggplant-Cheese Rollups 124
  Lasagna with Cheese 128
  Sambousak (Cheese-and-Egg-Filled Dough) 39
  White Syrian Cheese 122
CHICKEN
  Apricot-Prune Chicken 112
  Chicken à la King 110
  Chicken and Potatoes 106
  Chicken and Spaghetti 108
  Chicken and Stuffed Eggplant 107
  Chicken in Phyllo 22
  Chicken Pot Pie 105
  Chicken Sesame 109
  Chicken Soup 51
  Oven-Fried Chicken 109
  Poultry Stuffing 111
  Split Pea Soup with Chicken 53
  To clean chicken 16
CHICKPEAS
  Keskassoon 127
  Rice with Chickpeas 66
  Tomato and Chickpea Salad 46
Chile Con Carne 89
Chocolate Chip Cookies 155
Chocolate Mousse 149

INDEX

Chocolate Mousse Pie 150
COOKIES
    Chocolate Chip Cookies 155
    Dairy Rugelach 176
    Date Cakes 157
    Graybeh (Butter Ring Cookies) 151
    Hamantashen 159
    Ka'ak-Ib-Loz (Almond-Pistachio Rings) 162
    Krabeeg (Marshmallow Fluff Cookies) 164
    Mamoule (Nut-Filled Cookies) 167
    Passover Pistachio Cookies 174
    Suttlage Fingers (Cornstarch Pudding Pastries) 178
    Sweek Ka'ak (Crackers) 163
    Thumb-Print Cookies 180
Coconut Candy 158
Corned Beef and Cabbage, Pickled 88
Corn-Stuffed Tomatoes 81
Cream Cheese Cake 151
Creamed Cauliflower and Broccoli 75
CRÊPES
    Basic Crêpes 123
    Jibbon (Spinach Soufflé) in Crêpes 131
    Manicotti Crêpes 129
    Orange Crêpes 168
COMPOTE
    Mixed Berries Salad 175
    Strawberry Compote 179
Crumb Cake 153
Custard, Caramel Flan 154

D

DAIRY DISHES
    Baked Shells in Tomato Sauce 133
    Basic Crêpes 123
    Blintz Soufflé 121
    Bulgur with Cheese 121
    Creamed Cauliflower and Broccoli 75
    Eggplant-Cheese Rollups 124

    Eggplant Parmesan in Tomato Sauce 125
    Jibbon (Spinach Soufflé) in Crêpes 131
    Kelsonaise (Cheese Ravioli) 126
    Lasagna with Cheese 128
    Manicotti Crêpes 129
    Mechshe B'leban (Dairy Zucchini Stuffed with Rice) 137
    Noodle Pudding 130
    Sambousak (Cheese-and-Egg-Filled Dough) 39
    Spaghetti Primavera 132
    Spinach Phyllo 38
    Spinach Ravioli 134
    Ziti and Eggplant 135
    Zucchini Parmesan 136
Dairy Rugelach 176
Date and Nut Bread 148
Date Cakes 157
Deep Dish Peach Pie 171
DESSERTS
    Almasyia (Cornstarch Pudding) 145
    Apple Crisp 142
    Apple Pie 141
    Apricot Candy 144
    Ataiyef (Stuffed Pancakes) 143
    Baklava 147
    Bizzard (Roasted Pumpkin Seeds) 148
    Blueberry Muffins 146
    Bread Pudding 145
    Caramel Custard Flan 154
    Carrot Cake 156
    Cheese Danish 152
    Chocolate Chip Cookies 155
    Chocolate Mousse 149
    Chocolate Mousse Pie 150
    Coconut Candy 158
    Cream Cheese Cake 151
    Crumb Cake 153
    Dairy Rugelach 176

Date Cakes 157
Deep Dish Peach Pie 171
Fruit Tart 181
Graham Cracker Roll 158
Graybeh (Butter Ring Cookies) 151
Hamantashen 159
Heavenly Hash 166
Ka'ak-Ib-Loz (Almond-Pistachio Rings) 162
Kanafe (Shredded Dough) 160
Kanafe Ring 161
Krabeeg (Marshmallow Fluff Cookies) 164
Lemon Meringue Pie 165
Mamoule (Nut-Filled Cookies) 167
Mixed Berries Salad 175
Orange Crêpes 168
Orange Fantasia 169
Passover Nut Cake 170
Passover Pistachio Cookies 174
Pecan Pie 172
Pineapple Nut Cake 173
Rice Pudding 175
Sponge Cake 179
Strawberry Compote 179
Strawberry Shortcake 177
Suttlage Fingers (Cornstarch Pudding Pastries) 178
Sweet Ka'ak 163
Thumbprint Cookies 180
Tropical Fruit Salad 170
Dough — see Egg Roll Dough; Phyllo

E

Edgeh, Fried (Meat Omelet) 91
EGGPLANT
   Baba Ghanouj (Eggplant and Tahini Salad) 23
   Chicken and Stuffed Eggplant 107
   Eggplant-Cheese Rollups 124
   Eggplant Mechshe (Stuffed Eggplant) 90
   Eggplant Parmesan in Tomato Sauce 125
   Eggplant Salad 25
   Ratatouille on Toast 77
   Stuffed Eggplant Rolls 86
   Ziti and Eggplant 135
EGG ROLL DOUGH
   Egg Roll Dough 13
   Egg Rolls 26
   Empanadas 27
   Information about egg roll dough 13
   Kelsonaise (Cheese Ravioli) 126
   Spinach Ravioli 134
Empanadas 27

F

Fava Bean Salad 43
FISH
   Baked Whitefish 117
   Broiled Fillet of Sole 116
   Broiled Salmon 117
   Fish with Tahini 115
   Kibbe Matzah (with Fish Filling for Pesach) 30
   Salmon or Tuna Fish Cakes 118
   Whitefish Salad 48
Fresh Basil Sauce (for Pasta) 60
Fried Edgeh (Meat Omelet) 91
Fried Rice 66
FRUIT
   Apple Crisp 142
   Apple Pie 141
   Blueberry Muffins 146
   Deep Dish Peach Pie 171
   Fruit Tart 181
   Mixed Berries Salad 175
   Orange Crêpes 168
   Orange Fantasia 169
   Strawberry Compote 179
   Strawberry Shortcake 177
   Tropical Fruit Salad 170

INDEX

To peel tomatoes and peaches 15
To section oranges and grapefruits 15

G
Gazpacho 56
Graham Cracker Roll 158
Grape Leaves, Stuffed 93
Graybeh (Butter Ring Cookies) 151
Great Northern Beans 73
Green Beans and Veal 78
Green Beans with Egg 78
GREEN PEPPERS
   Green Pepper, Onion, and Tomato Mechshe 92
   Pickled Green Peppers 35

H
Hamantashen 159
Heavenly Hash 166

J
Jibbon (Spinach Soufflé) in Crêpes 131

K
Ka'ak, Sweet 163
Ka'ak-Ib-Loz (Almond-Pistachio Rings) 162
Kanafe (Shredded Dough) 160
Kanafe Ring 161
Keftes (Syrian Meatball Sauce) 59
Kelsonaise (Cheese Ravioli) 126
Keskassoon 127
KIBBE
   Information about kibbe meat 14
   Kibbe Balls (Meatballs) 61
   Kibbe Homda Sauce 60
   Kibbe Matzah (with Fish Filling for Pesach) 30
   Kibbe Neye 37
   Kibbe Torpedoes 29
   Kibbe with Vegetable Filling 31
   Rolled Kibbe with Cherries 94

Shurba (Rice Soup with Kibbe) 55
Knishes, Potato (in Phyllo) 28
Krabeeg (Marshmallow Fluff Cookies) 164
Krefsiah (Swiss Chard) 82

L
Lahemageen (Meat Pizza) 32
Lasagna with Cheese 128
Lemon Meringue Pie 165
Lemon Sauce (Bedab Lemuna) 62
LENTILS
   Ades (Red Lentil Soup) 52
   Lentil-Noodle Soup 52
   M'gedrah (Lentils and Rice) 67
   Lubyeh (Black-Eyed Peas) 76

M
Mamoule (Nut-Filled Cookies) 167
Manicotti Crêpes 129
Margarine — *to clarify margarine or butter* 15
Matzah Balls 55
Meat — *see also Chicken*
MEAT
   Beef Stroganoff 85
   Bestell (Meat-Filled Dough) 21
   Blehat (Meat Stuffed with Egg) 19
   Chile Con Carne 89
   Eggplant Mechshe (Stuffed Eggplant) 90
   Empanadas 27
   Fried Edgeh (Meat Omelet) 91
   Green Beans and Veal 78
   Green Pepper, Onion, and Tomato Mechshe 92
   Keftes (Syrian Meatball Sauce) 59
   Kibbe Torpedoes 29
   Lahemageen (Meat Pizza) 32
   Lubyeh (Black-Eyed Peas) 76
   Pepper Steak 97

Pickled Corned Beef and Cabbage 88
Rolled Kibbe with Cherries 94
Shish Kebab 99
Shurba (Rice Soup with Kibbe) 55
Stuffed Breast of Veal with Mushrooms 101
Stuffed Cabbage 87
Stuffed Eggplant Rolls 86
Stuffed Grape Leaves 93
Stuffed Zucchini 102
Sul Ajon (Ground Meat on a Skewer) 99
Sweet-and-Sour Meatballs 96
Sweet-and-Sour Tongue 98
Sweetbreads and Mushrooms 95
Veal Française 100

Meatballs, Sweet and Sour 96
M'gedrah (Lentils and Rice) 67
MECHSHE
   Chicken and Stuffed Eggplant 107
   Eggplant-Cheese Rollups 125
   Eggplant Mechshe (Stuffed Eggplant) 90
   Green Pepper, Onion, and Tomato Mechshe 92
   Mechshe B'leban (Dairy Zucchini Stuffed with Rice) 137
   Stuffed Cabbage 87
   Stuffed Grape Leaves 93
   Stuffed Mushrooms 79
   Stuffed Zucchini (meat) 102
Mint Leaves — *to dry fresh mint leaves* 16
Mixed Berries Salad 175
Mock Tamarind Sauce 62
MOUSSE
   Chocolate Mousse 149
   Chocolate Mousse Pie 150
Muffins, Blueberry 146
MUSHROOMS
   Mushroom Turnovers 33
   Pickled Mushrooms 34
   Stuffed Breast of Veal with Mushrooms 101
   Stuffed Mushrooms 79
   Sweetbreads and Mushrooms 95

N

Noodles — see Pasta
Noodles with Tahini 127
NUTS
   Ataiyef (Stuffed Pancakes) 143
   Baklava 147
   Bizzard (Roasted Pumpkin Seeds) 148
   Chocolate Chip Cookies 155
   Date and Nut Bread 148
   Dairy Rugelach 176
   Ka'ak-Ib-Loz (Almond-Pistachio Rings) 162
   Krabeeg (Marshmallow Fluff Cookies) 164
   Mamoule (Nut-Filled Cookies) 167
   Passover Nut Cake 170
   Passover Pistachio Cookies 174
   Pecan Pie 172
   Pineapple Nut Cake 173
   Rice with Nuts 65
   Thumbprint Cookies 180
   To toast nuts 15

O

Onion Soup 54
Onion, Tomato, and Green Pepper Mechshe 92
ORANGES
   Orange Crêpes 168
   Orange Fantasia 169
   To section oranges and grapefruits 15
Orange Water, *information about* 14
Orzo Salad 44

INDEX

Oven-Fried Chicken 109

P
PARMESAN
    Eggplant Parmesan in Tomato Sauce 125
    Zucchini Parmesan 136
Passover Nut Cake 170
Passover Pistachio Cookies 174
PASTA
    Baked Shells in Tomato Sauce 133
    Chicken and Spaghetti 108
    Fresh Basil Sauce (for Pasta) 60
    Keskassoon 127
    Lasagna with Cheese 128
    Lentil-Noodle Soup 52
    Noodle Pudding 130
    Noodles with Tahini 127
    Spaghetti Primavera 132
Peas, Black Eyed (Lubyeh) 76
Pecan Pie 172
Pepper Steak 97
Pickled Corned Beef and Cabbage 88
PICKLES
    Pickled Artichokes 34
    Pickled Cabbage 36
    Pickled Carrots 35
    Pickled Cauliflower 36
    Pickled Green Peppers 35
    Pickled Mushrooms 34
    Pickled Turnips 36
PHYLLO
    Baklava 147
    Chicken in Phyllo 22
    Information about phyllo dough 14
    Spinach Phyllo 38
    Suttlage Fingers 178
PIES
    Apple Pie 141
    Chicken Pot Pie 105
    Chocolate Mousse Pie 150
    Deep Dish Peach Pie 171
    Lemon Meringue Pie 165
    Pecan Pie 172
Pignolia Nuts, *information about* 14
Pineapple Nut Cake 173
POTATOES
    Baked Fried Potatoes 80
    Chicken and Potatoes 106
    Potato Knishes in Phyllo 28
    Red Skin Potato Salad 45
    Roast Potatoes 80
Poultry — see Chicken
Poultry Stuffing 111
PUDDING
    Almasyia (Cornstarch Pudding) 145
    Bread Pudding 145
    Noodle Pudding 130
    Rice Pudding 175
Pumpkin Seeds, Roasted (Bizzard) 148

R
Ratatouille on Toast 77
RAVIOLI
    Kelsonaise (Cheese Ravioli) 126
    Spinach Ravioli 134
Red Lentil Soup (Ades) 52
Red Skin Potato Salad 45
RICE
    Fried Rice 66
    M'gedrah (Lentils and Rice) 67
    Plain Rice 65
    Rice with Orzo 65
    Rice Pudding 175
    Rice with Chickpeas 66
    Rice with Nuts 65
    Rice with Peas 68
    Shurba (Rice Soup with Kibbe) 55
    Spanish Rice 68

Roast Potatoes 80
Rolled Kibbe with Cherries 94
Rugelach, Dairy 176

S

SALADS
    Baba Ghanouj (Eggplant and Tahini Salad) 23
    Bazaghan (Cracked Wheat Salad) 20
    Caesar Salad 43
    Eggplant Salad 25
    Fava Bean Salad 43
    Orzo Salad 44
    Red Skin Potato Salad 45
    Salata (Chopped Syrian Salad) 48
    Tabouli (Cracked Wheat with Vegetables) 47
    Tomato and Chickpea Salad 46
    Whitefish Salad 48
Salata (Chopped Syrian Salad) 48
Salmon, Broiled 117
Salmon Fish Cakes 118
Sambousak (Cheese-and-Egg-Filled Dough) 39
SAUCES
    Bedab Lemuna (Lemon Sauce) 62
    Fresh Basil Sauce (for Pasta) 60
    Keftes (Syrian Meatball Sauce) 59
    Kibbe Homda Sauce 60
    Mock Tamarind Sauce 62
Shish Kebab 99
Shurba (Rice Soup with Kibbe) 55
SOUPS
    Ades (Red Lentil Soup) 52
    Chicken Soup 51
    Gazpacho 56
    Lentil-Noodle Soup 52
    Matzah Balls 55
    Onion Soup 54
    Shurba (Rice Soup with Kibbe) 55

    Split Pea Soup with Chicken 53
Spaghetti — see Pasta
Spaghetti Primavera 132
Spanish Rice 68
Spinach Phyllo 38
Spinach Ravioli 134
Spinach Soufflé, in Crêpes (Jibbon) 131
Split Pea Soup with Chicken 53
Sponge Cake 179
Strawberry Compote 179
Strawberry Shortcake 177
Stuffed Breast of Veal with Mushrooms 101
Stuffed Cabbage 87
Stuffed Eggplant Rolls 86
Stuffed Grape Leaves 93
Stuffed Mushrooms 79
Stuffed Vegetables — see Mechshe
Stuffed Zucchini 102
Stuffing, Poultry 111
Sul Ajon (Ground Meat on a Skewer) 99
Suttlage Fingers (Cornstarch Pudding Pastries) 178
Sweet-and-Sour Meatballs 96
Sweet-and-Sour Tongue 98
Sweetbreads and Mushrooms 95
Sweet Ka'ak (Crackers) 163
Swiss Chard (Krefsiah) 82

T

Tabouli (Cracked Wheat with Vegetables) 47
TAHINI
    Baba Ghanouj (Eggplant and Tahini Salad) 23
    Fish with Tahini 115
    Information about tahini 14
    Noodles with Tahini 127

    Tahini Dip 40
TAMARIND
    Information about tamarind 14
    Mock Tamarind Sauce 62
Tart, Fruit 181
Thumbprint Cookies 180
TOMATOES
    Corn-Stuffed Tomatoes 81
    Gazpacho 56
    Tomato and Chickpea Salad 46
    Tomato and Egg 82
    Tomato, Green Pepper, and Onion Mechshe 92
    To peel tomatoes and peaches 15
Tongue, Sweet and Sour 98
Torpedoes, Kibbe 29
Tropical Fruit Salad 170
Tuna Fish Cakes 118

V

VEAL
    Green Beans and Veal 78
    Stuffed Breast of Veal with Mushrooms 101
    Veal Française 100
VEGETABLES
    Artichoke Medias (Stuffed Artichoke Hearts) 71
    Artichokes in Oil 72
    Asparagus Winter 72
    Baked Carrots 73
    Baked Fried Potatoes 80
    Carrot Ring 74
    Corn-Stuffed Tomatoes 81
    Creamed Cauliflower and Broccoli 75
    Great Northern Beans 73
    Green Beans and Veal 78
    Green Beans with Egg 78
    Krefsiah (Swiss Chard) 82
    Ratatouille on Toast 77
    Roast Potatoes 80
    Stuffed Mushrooms 79
    Tomato and Egg 82

W

WHITEFISH
    Baked Whitefish 117
    Whitefish Salad 48
White Syrian Cheese 122

Z

Ziti and Eggplant 135
ZUCCHINI
    Mechshe B'leban (Dairy Zucchini Stuffed with Rice) 137
    Ratatouille on Toast 77
    Stuffed Zucchini (Meat) 102
    Zucchini Parmesan 136

About the author: When Rae Dayan's parents came to America from Allepo, Syria, they brought with them their collection of Sephardic recipes dating back generations. As a little girl, Rae loved to observe her mother's nimble fingers shaping delicacy after delicacy. The compliments on the food abounded at everyday meals, on Shabbat, and on all happy occasions.

As a young bride, Rae would consult her mother or any other expert she could find to sharpen her culinary skills. Many years later she passed on the knowledge and heritage to a new generation of young brides by offering beginner courses in Sephardic cooking and baking.

Rae Dayan's skills — and her recipes — have been applauded in the *New York Times, Hadassah Magazine, Kosher Gourmet*, and many other publications.